Gail Simmons
My Godfather +
Dad's roommate at
Hotchkiss + Yale

Adventures and Misadventures

Adventures and Misadventures

The Life and Some of the Times
of George W. Carrington, USMC

George W. Carrington,
Col., USMC (Ret.), D. Phil., Oxon.

VANTAGE PRESS
New York

To the Marine Military Academy
Where the Finest Education for the Most Deserving
of Young Men Is Offered in the Most Elite of Atmospheres

Contents

Illustrations

Foreword

Colonel George Carrington's life has been nothing short of an exciting adventure. He communicates his unusual experiences, introduces the reader to unforgettable relationships he forged throughout the years, and takes us on a unique journey relating many of "the good, the bad, and the ugly" encounters in his insightful, informative, and highly entertaining book.

I value and respect his comments and observations on earlier Marine Corps combat commitments. Through the campaigns or crises of his generation—Bougainville, Guam, Iwo Jima, North China, Korea, Taiwan, and Vietnam—he leads any student of history from a unique vantage point as the pages reveal his first-hand account of combat trials and victories. His tribute to enlisted Marines, especially to those who bear the brunt of combat in the infantry, reveals an uncompromising, unbiased and honest evaluation of a true leader. He tells us that Marines, like good fathers, teachers, preachers, coaches, and even policemen, serve society by taking care of their subordinates. Although many of his experiences in combat were prior to my own, his stories, criticisms, and praising of particular episodes of bravery and self-sacrifice in Vietnam were specially relevant and of particular interest to me, having served two combat tours there myself.

His remarks on training, discipline, and leadership are right on the mark. His treatment of racial or ethnic equality, moral behavior, and underlying spirituality is unapologetically straightforward and positive. He takes us through his start in life, his pride in being a Marine, his peacetime experience in the Far East,

Quantico, Camp Lejeune, and Washington, D.C., his valuable pursuits and achievements in education, and finally, his arrival at pleasant retirement. Colonel Carrington's book takes the reader on the journey of a life well spent—with undoubtedly many more adventures ahead.

It was my distinct honor and privilege to have joined Colonel Carrington's journey here at the Marine Military Academy in Harlingen, Texas, when I became president several years ago. Not only was he father of a previous cadet, but he also had served as academic dean. He became an advisor and helped our institution as a long-serving trustee. I applaud the dedication of a man who excels at everything he attempts. This book is just one more example.

Wayne E. Rollings
Major General, U.S. Marine Corps (Ret.)
President, Marine Military Academy

Preface

I have contemplated how to design a pattern to this account of growing up, stumbling into the career of a Marine, the lucky chance of becoming a regular, and the fortunate steps that progressed to great adventures in the most interesting of times. I intended it as a memoir, but inevitably it turned into an autobiography. I seek to muse on matters, follow a theme, overlook much, forget about research, and speak in my own voice. And the musing is to be concentrated upon matters military—and, yes, naval. How pertinent it is to remember that we are known as Soldiers of the Sea. I read that Marines were first put aboard ships in order to protect the captain from possible mutineers.

One should not jump around too much, forward and back. Family and childhood must come first. However, as I progress through topics or subjects, I sometimes have to repeat visits to certain places, diverting from a strictly chronological approach. I digress a bit and necessarily find myself returning to locations and the persons involved. An author does not want to overlook either the important and consequential, or the trivial and entertaining. It is best to keep your eye on the doughnut, but do not let anything escape through the hole.

It is natural to laud one's heroes, one's betters. I hope I disguise identity of those about whom I am critical. I like to be perverse. I occasionally discover seeming problems that could have been regarded as solutions. I sometimes hint that I think that some of my superiors did not always perform perfectly. I include some stories that do not reflect the favorable. Occasionally I joke or second-guess. There have to be those placed in command of others; sometimes mistakes are made.

A winning characteristic of Mark Twain's writing was to tell it in the vernacular. He shocked many in his day, but his work "told it how it is." So relax with me as I declare that I'm gonna do what I wanna do. Ain't it okay to use contractions? Sometimes the heck with quotation marks. You'll savvy my slang.

Of course, I am writing, composing, a narrative to be read, not listened to as speech. However, I throw in, too, as a matter of communication, how instructors were trained to lecture at Marine Corps Schools, Quantico. We called it "Charm School." We all must be irritated or diverted when hearing, "You know, I mean, you know, what I am trying to say, you know, I mean, you know"—they call 'em verbal pauses. Too, so often do we hear the double negative that I know you will sympathize when I assert that I'm sometimes not gonna be obedient, subservient, respectful to nobody. No way.

I love aphorisms. I hope I can conjure them up usefully along the way. One applicable today, is, "You Always Have To Employ More Force Than Is Necessary." Certainly this is true in combat, at war. However, I'll concede that "always" has to be altered to "sometimes," thinking about police action and resultant police abuse. Another, important for warriors and politicians, is "Bluffs Come Home To Haunt You." And, for dictators and autocrats, "Tell Me What I Want to Hear." It has been said that the first Casualty of War is the Truth. Yet the easiest way of all is to speak or write the Truth. As my father once told me, "I have never made a mistake. They were always my choices or decisions. So they cannot be mistakes. But I do admit that they sometimes had bad results."

Adventures and Misadventures

ONE
Family and Childhood

I emerged on the scene in Manhattan, that islet known as New York. I have always heard that my 1921 birthplace was Sloan's Baby Hospital, and I have borne that babyish stigma lo these many decades. I start now on this autobiographical story that I hope has the character of a memoir. It is intended to be masculine, military, and naval, but I must commence with my childhood.

My earliest home was an apartment in Greenwich Village, although my parents probably never knew it as such. When my mother observed that I was inordinately interested in picking up cigarette and cigar butts in Washington Square, the decision was reached to move out to Westchester County. I proudly proclaim Westchester's capital as White Plains, and I now conjure up memory of Gen. George Washington's early confrontation with the British redcoats at the Battle of White Plains. We Carringtons alighted for a short time in Bronxville, a good Dutch name, but eventually established our home in Scarsdale. Sunny Scarsdale, I call it. We were then a Carrington family of five, my two sisters following in my trace.

*   *   *

Of great importance in my life, was Pops, my father. He was George Williams C. and that makes me "junior." I have never liked that appendage, but it was not until I entered the naval service and obtained a rank that I could drop it. He was from

1

Charleston, South Carolina, where they used to say that the Ashley and Cooper rivers came together to form the Atlantic Ocean. In his boyhood home and during the Great Depression his parents gave care and a living to ex-slaves, including Jacob, suffering from diabetes. So, I ventured south to my grandparents' Charleston, where I was once dispatched for a Christmas vacation. One winter after coming down with a surprise case of chicken pox, I was sentenced to attend an all-girls' school, an unpleasant memory.

Grandmother reigned supreme in their home at Number Two Meeting Street, from which you could sight President Abraham's worrisome islet of Sumter. Grandfather, with first name of Waring, was mild, pleasant, liked to take me to the movies. I was impressed by his tremendous breakfasts—including pigs' feet, hominy grits, kippers, eggs, and sausage. Sunday luncheons were grim, with many guests and lasting until 4:00 or 5:00 P.M. It was said that my grandfather had been a drummer boy in "The Late Unpleasantness Between The States." My powerhouse grandmother never addressed him by that first name, but as "Mr. Carrington."

She directed Jacob to hobble every day to the market, usually for fish, not meat; for refrigeration in the South was then practically non-existent. Her colored cook who was once asked how much dressing or seasoning she was adding replied, "bout a mowf full." The chauffeur, Carol, took me once to the barber, after which it appeared that a bowl had been fitted on me, topside. Carol was accused of having had a drink and Grandmother fired him. Replacements were interviewed, maybe a dozen of them, black and white, in this Depression time, for a job of perhaps twenty bucks a month. I felt so sorry for each and all of them and wanted all to be hired.

My forefathers, Charleston-side, were good to the blacks, gave them help and home, and founded the first and best orphanage for them after the Civil War. And, one can say, the slavers, the ship captains, who orignally brought the blacks from Africa, were largely New England Yankees. I might have been exposed to privilege, but with my family background I was also learning compassion, care, responsibility, and conscience.

*   *   *

My mother, Helen, would usually say she came from Cincinnati, but there is something to add here. Her family name was Graydon, and Graydons came from County Monahan, in the north of Ireland. One summer my grandmother having borne eight children already in Cincinnati, Ohio, USA, was perhaps a little inattentive to the calendar, and my mother came into the world in Ireland. The family wisecrack over the years in answer to the question, does not that make her Irish? was "Just because the cat had its kittens in the oven does not make them muffins."

Grandfather Graydon got hit in the eye by a cricket ball at Trinity College in Dublin. This restricted his vision to the degree that his education was interrupted and so he, not the first-born in the system of primogeniture, emigrated via Canada to the U.S. He made it pretty well in Cincinnati. He flourished in the Gilded Age, starting with a kind of Lydia Pinkham patent medicine but probably expanding thereafter into other ventures in our booming nation. His many descendants (including me) could consider themselves lucky. I was to seek a manly course in life, yet I know that a complete man should have a feminine hint to his makeup. Well, trouble was insofar as I was concerned, there was too much of the feminine for me—grandmas, mother, sisters, aunts, girl cousins, sissies—on my Cincinnati-side.

*   *   *

So how did my parents meet? What did Cincinnati have to do with Charleston? I have sometimes been asked that question, and I give an answer that offers a bit of interesting history. In the summer of 1914 my Charleston grandparents embarked upon a cruise that must have been rare in that day. The participants included my father, his sister, and her schoolmate friend. Alongside them in a Norwegian fjord they spotted *Hohenzollern,* the yacht of Kaiser Wilhelm, and some German naval escorts. Next morning the flotilla had vanished. The family story told me was that this was the very time of the assassination of Archduke Ferdinand in Sarajevo, leading to the outbreak of World War I. That assassination was in fact on June 28th. Historical accounts have it that the volatile and aggressive Kaiser was sequestered at Kiel, sailing his yacht, to keep him quiet and out of the picture. However, enquiry into the work of John Keegan, the eminent historian of WW I, reveals that from 6 to 26 July Kaiser Wilhelm was on his yacht for his annual three-week cruise in the Norwegian fjords. Perhaps it was Monday, 27 July, that he returned to Germany! My grandparents and family traveled on, ignorant of world developments. They landed in Denmark and roosted in the southwestern port of Esbjerg, to await a butter boat to get them out to Halifax, England. It was home for his finish of college and the naval service for my father. It was the initial meeting for my mother, the schoolmate friend, and the man she was to marry.

*   *   *

As a ten-year-old I was conscious that Herbert Hoover had been president. However, I hint of Franklin Delano Roosevelt in recalling a memory of a campaign button which read, "Spread the News, Goodbye Blues. Happy New Year, 1932." Repeal of Prohibition was represented as a wonderful deal for adults. Friends calling on my parents were either shocked or amused by my emphasis in identifying the day of the week as, "Sunday, the day my Pops makes gin." In my emergence into the FDR era in the very Republican village of Scarsdale, New York, kids reflecting their parents' attitudes proclaimed that the NRA of President Roosevelt's Na-

4

tional Recovery Act really meant "Nuts Running America." If one was from Charleston, indeed he found himself a lonely Democrat.

Scarsdale, my part of town, included a "Chinaman." This dignified Chinese gentleman, living in an middle-class home and section of town, was one day washing his car. It was a neat target for mud and horse turds, flung by me and my pals. He called the cops on us. One guy imaginatively but immaterially pleaded, "You can't arrest me. My mother is having a nervous breakdown!" When one recalls this episode, there springs to mind the ditty "Ching, Ching, Chinaman, sitting on a fence, trying to make a dollar out of fifteen cents." And another, "Paddy was an Irishman, Paddy was a thief . . ." Thus were some of the racial attitudes of that day, in Sunny Scarsdale. How do such ditties migrate, among children, through generations, across vast distances?

Religion? Church did not matter importantly in my boyhood, I report honestly. At the annual Memorial Day parade the Boy Scouts were strictly ordered not to tread on the graves at St. James the Less Episcopal Church. Sunday school was conducted by the father of a pal and is best remembered for the delight of escape by climbing out the window. Then one could climb the very tall pine tree on the church grounds to a height from which on a clear day you could glimpse the tallest buildings in New York City. Confirmation instruction into the Church was shallow. It was conducted briefly, squeezed in before one had to head back to boarding school. Yet today the Church is solidly with me. It has always been there to give me security and tranquility. I do not try real hard to conjure up my sins, so they stay minimal or unacknowledged. My parents could not credit nor escape blame for this. Their attendance at church was just occasional. But later in our lives the Church has been an essential part in the very salvation of my beloved life companion, Else.

Scarsdale schools were Edgewood, Edgemont, Greenacres, and Fox Meadow, pretty descriptive names. The poor guys from Edgemont were ineligible for Scarsdale High. They had to travel to Bronxville for high school. But Bronxville had a movie theatre; Scarsdale, none. Bronxville was where Joe Kennedy settled his brood, commuting to Manhattan and down to Wall Street. This enabled Robert one day to contend that New York State had once been his residence, when he ran for his Senate seat.

Images of Edgewood remain. It had great opportunities for recess, somehow an important consideration. I knew the gym where we attempted not jump shots, but the underhand shot of that day. I do not remember learning much in the classroom, probably why my parents were to pop me into my next step for schooling. However, in Music Appreciation we were guided into acquiring zithers. Too, we learned that "A Penny Earned is a Penny Saved," by starting savings accounts at two percent interest. My father, scolding me for allowing the lights to burn unnecessarily, had a variation: "Do you think money grows on trees?"

After World War I in the navy he worked on Wall Street, probably in a job arranged by influential friends. He reported once that in an effort to acquire a raise, he got, "Carrington, don't you realize how much prestige you enjoy in Brown Brothers, Harriman?" His reply, although I do not believe he really dared voice it, but it makes a good story, "Yes—but I can't eat prestige."

I must tell of Scarsdale now in explanation of How It Was, then; or of what created or influenced the nature of my generation in this admitted corner of privilege. Scarsdale was neat, as they used to say. We had sports, which started with my Pops, who played catch with me. Sports get a guy off to a masculine beginning. They are linked to memory of Edgewood School, aptly named for its location near woods. Once "wops" from "Guineaville," properly Eastchester, deliberately set a fire in these woods. We called the cops and firemen. Later the "wops" cornered me and threatened to throw me into a water-filled quarry. It remains a rare, remembered instance of fear in my childhood. But I could run and took refuge in the village barbershop with my protector therein.

In Scarsdale there were not many Italians and Irish, that is to classify them—Catholics. An Italian ran the liquor store after we emerged from Prohibition. Brothers, indeed themselves named Irish, were stars on the village of Scarsdale football team and ran the butcher shop. Once we had a so-called track meet of the kids of the Episcopal, Congregational, and Catholic churches. The Italian and Irish kids won everything. They called their coach "Father." I wondered why. My father was Pops, in my home. "Sisters" ran their school. My sisters lived with me on Circle Road, where it intersected with Overhill, both good names. Circle Road provided a great opportunity to ride in the horse-drawn milk wagon around the circle. You could pick up horse turds to throw at any enemies. Also, Circle Road was good for a ride on his motorcycle with the Spanish gardener (really Spanish and not from Mexico as most are in my retirement home in California).

I do not think we were prejudiced in those days. I was puzzled one day by being told I must be Jewish. Why? "Because you part your hair in the middle." We WASPs strongly outnumbered the Catholics. However, I only recall differentiating by my mother's emphasis upon *Roman* Cs.

There was one serious theme or current developing within me at this early age. Call it consciousness of others, the outside world. The Japanese moved into Manchuria in 1931, precipitating the decline of the influence of the League of Nations. Later Japs took over in North China, destined to be very important for me, and Mussolini and his Italians decided to invade Ethiopia. It was conjectured that they would not succeed because their vehicles would run out of gas. Next came Hitler. Others my age might have also been aware of these outside events, but I sincerely claim that my interest and concern was greater than that of my buddies. I was to progress through other schools and gravitate to majoring in European History at Dear Old Yale. I am permitted here to get ahead of my story because this was truly a tide or direction that was defining to my life and career. European, American, Chinese, and Japanese History were to come. Ultimately I topped all this off at Oxford.

Scarsdale was fun. I recall it as challenging, joyous, and adventurous. I guess it was just boyish. We had bikes, My father had me rake leaves and clean out gutters, heck, they do not even have gutters where I live today! I preferred the company of the boys and brothers of other families and seemed to prefer times in their households over my own. The Boy Scouts were an important additive to school. There had been the Cub Scouts at first, but they did not count. Too babyish. We learned to march, stand at attention, make a fire, earn merit badges, and recite the Scout oath. I took the Boy Scouts seriously and I treasure memory of their jamborees and going up to West Point with them to see the first football game of the year. I picked up something, however, that might be regarded as a handicap—I could not tell a lie. I did not learn this from George Washington or in church, but perhaps a bit from family and schools and certainly and most positively from the Boy Scouts of America.

*   *   *

At a summer camp for boys in New Hampshire to which I was sent, I was introduced to rifle marksmanship, to archery, to swimming in a cold lake, and, most importantly, to putting on the boxing gloves and getting in the ring. I was not very good, but I was tall and the sport was a challenge. I was eventually to find myself on the Yale freshman boxing team, 175-lb. spot. Here we go again to West Point. Gerry Ford was our coach—yes, the same Ford who years later was to become president. He nurse-maided us along on the bus from New Haven to West Point to the Thayer Hotel (as in Sylvanus Thayer and Alfred Thayer Mahan). I had sparred with him, then probably at law school and more renowned at Michigan football than Yale pugilism. We Yalies, from urban, dirty old New Haven, were overwhelmed if not by our ring opponents but by what went on at a winter weekend at West Point. The cadets had all invited dates, to their Hop. The Prom. The Band. Cheering thunderously for the home team. There was varsity boxing, wrestling, hockey, basketball, and swimming. The varsity boxers and wrestlers were about seven years older than I, having been to other colleges prior to West Point. They already bore prominent names and reputations for their football prowess. Looking aross the gym, I thought, *Migod, next year I'll be in their league!* It was near the end of boxing for me. In any case, I probably only belonged on the eighth floor of the Yale gym, sparring with Gerry Ford.

Getting back to Sunny Scarsdale: how do ships, sailors, Marines, the United States Navy also get into my story? My pal Jack, from the Edgemont section of Scarsdale, had a father who told his son to put up his dukes and spar with him. Tough guy Jack would tell us, "When you come up here, across the tracks, to Edgemont, to Old Army Road, you gotta fight!" But there was a more enjoyable occasion to come, out of acquainance with Jack. He had a grandfather who was an admiral on board the *Maryland,* a battleship visiting on the Hudson River. We got to hear the band play and see the Marine Detachment on parade on the fantail at sunset. It is a stunning, beautiful, remembered scene. Jack should have joined the Marine Corps instead of the navy, and stayed in the service.

*   *   *

Summertime, when the living was easy, too easy for my preference, meant Marion, Massachusetts, where we had a summer pad. It was named after Francis Marion, the "Swamp Fox," who bedeviled the Brits in the Revolutionary War. It is said that this name for a community occurs in more states of the nation than any other. Marion is on Buzzards Bay, also an interesting name, near Cape Cod and seedy old New Bedford.

My father knew it out of acquaintances from school, college,

9

or the navy. We enjoyed ownership of what was known as the superintendent's house. Other original homes included the gate house, the farmer's home, the laundry, the fire station with its high tower, the ice house, and the stables, which became the garage. Yachts were moored at the pier adjacent to the mansion, gone in my time but once so grand that guests were assigned to rooms by number as at a hotel. There were several new homes, meandering roads and driveways, massive stands of rhododendrons, tennis courts, and beach houses. And the empty part of the woods was where the Deer Park once flourished.

My Pops got minimum return from this over the years. He had to work five-and-a-half days a week in distant Manhattan, where he had to wear a stiff collar and got only two weeks' vacation a year. I was surrounded by Mother, grandmothers, aunts, sisters, and girl cousins—a sissy society. I was limited in many ways. "No, you cannot go in swimming until two hours after a meal."

During the polio scare of the 30s we were instructed as we drove through a neighboring village, hardly a city, "Hold your noses and get down on the backseat floor as we pass through town." And several times, "No, I don't want you taking the rowboat out that far."

Today I recall that New Hampshire boys' camp, living in tents, rifle marksmanship, archery, canoeing, and little boys' boxing—certainly with pleasure equal or better than that associated with yachts, tennis courts, dancing school, and unnecessary trips to the doctors.

TWO

Schools and College

Arnold Toynbee, I recall, wrote that man thrives on challenges. Not too great, as the extremes of cold and heat stifle the Eskimo or one who endures the jungle—but just good, steady, exposure, competition, and maybe some struggle. I have mentioned the Boy Scouts and the New Hampshire camp, but one can really get his motor going at school. My parents decided that I would be prepared by being sent to what was called an "English," country day school. Prepared for what? Well, becoming a preppie, at the next step, termed a preparatory school. Beyond that? Well more later, but early on I unconsciously was seeking escape from captivity.

Repton (how English a name) was located at some distance from my hometown so we had to be rounded up in a dilapidated limousine, then termed a jitney. The driver was named Cypher, so we called him Zero. Zero was harassed some winter mornings by a mother who would peer down on the icy road to see if he had put on chains. He would calm down the horseplay and rambunctious behavior by engrossing us in guessing games—for example names of automobiles, movies, or states of the union. It was in the middle of the Great Depression, Zero could not have been paid much. Most of us boys realized that this schooling expense was a privilege, something extra being given to us by our parents.

The athletic program was O.K., but there were limitations. We did not take part in the great American game of football. Instead, soccer. Baseball took place on a slightly slanted diamond, the pitcher having to go a bit uphill, and the batter in "better box," shall we say. The so-called gym was once a garage, but I'll bet today that it was really made-over stables. We were shooed out on hikes in the winter, and we got home rather late, obliged then to get on with serious homework. After athletics, we changed in the cellar, with benches, hooks for clothing, and no-hot-water showers. We were a very small school, so everybody had to help on the first, second, or third teams. The soccer coach—I do not recall what course he taught—was an Annapolis graduate. That year in the Great Depression the United States of America decided it could only commission and afford to call to duty in the navy the top of each class. He was a good guy, getting the best alternative start on a career. Of course, he eventually got into the navy, but not very hot prospects of making captain or admiral someday, I'd say. In those years the navy had waiting lists for men to enlist. Call me an old grump, however I cannot but comment on today's scramble to get men aboard in the first place and bribery to reenlist.

Academics were more important. A shocker for me, coming in mid-year, was that I had to commence Latin and French. My eight or so classmates in what was termed Fourth Form surely had a start on me. I had a bit of catching up to do, from the contrast at Edgewood School where I had been judged by my report card on whether I waited my turn in line at the drinking fountain. We stood in rows and ranks by form, or class, at morning assembly, when the headmaster would scold, praise, and announce what was to come, sermonize, or comment on the wide world outside. Mondays were distinctive for a special ceremony. My second week I stumbled into one of the spots near the left end of my Fourth Form line, only to hear a buzzing or mumbling of protest from my classmates. Academic performance for the previous week was announced, and I found that I stood last and was supposed to stand at the right-end tail of things.

I improved, learning an important lesson about competition in study, as well as in athletics, and in life itself (Leo Durocher said it: "Nice guys finish last.") Years later, still a callow youth, 2nd Lt. USMCR, I discovered that for about 30 of us standing in ranks at morning assembly there were only 20 washbasins for a shave. I missed first day, but learned how to jump over the small hedge and beat it up the stairs so as not to be Tail-End Charlie. Yeah, and I recall another pal, of whom it was said that if there were 21 waiting in line to get into 20 seats on a bus, he'd be standing up every time. Repton revved up my first competitive instincts.

There is not much remembered about spiritual training in those Repton days. If there were morning prayers, I did not pay attention. Let Sunday school take care of that. Today there is one matter about which I belatedly confess. In Math, far short of quadratic equations, solving for unknowns, geometry, celestial navigation, calculus, in all of which I got pretty good—we were given numbers arranged in linear progression to straighten out. As a simple example, 4 plus 2, times 3, minus 8, divided by 2, considered in order, equal 5. Right? Try it. However, nobody had taught me that 4 plus (2 times 3) minus (8 divided by 2) equals 6. Try again, I jiggered things into correct solutions on more complex, number series from the answers on the torn-out pages of the math book I had hidden at home. I cheated. But again, nobody had taught me the correct way. If a sin, 'twas forgivable. In any case, Straight Arrow George has remembered this for lo these many years.

Allow me to return to spirituality at a later stage of my life. Morality as we began to pick it up at Repton was something else. Our headmaster termed himself Captain V. Willoughby Barrett, quite a handle. He was a gallant British veteran who had been gassed in Flanders during World War I, and accordingly had coughing fits that frequently forced him out of the classroom. Some mothers hissed that he probably retired to have a swig at the bottle, but we youngsters revered him. He wrote, "You are going on to fulfill the ideals of your parents and of your school. This means hard work, much hard work, much ambition and also the desire to do something for others." But this admired headmaster revealed one, dumb, anti-American attitude that my Pops countered in glorious fashion. At the time of the 1933 World Series, New York Yankees versus Washington Senators, he produced tickets for us! V. Willoughby announced, "Oh, no we don't allow absences for such a purpose. I would see that he gets zeroes for all his classes." My Pops dismissed him with "Go ahead!" We attended Yankee Stadium, and Pops earned another gold star of esteem in my book.

* * *

After little boys' school there came preparatory school, though I had not discovered for what I was preparing. It was for me, rather, a matter of predestination, as the Puritans used to put it. My father had been sent from Charleston, South Carolina, "Heart of the Old Confederacy," up to Yankee land to Hotchkiss School, in the northwest corner of Connecticut. Let me now admit it; Hotchkiss was preparatory to getting me into Yale. Before the Civil War, South Carolina was second after Connecticut in students there. John C. Calhoun, no less, had gone to Yale Law School, but after the War there was an absolute void in aspirations and decisions for Southerners to send their children north for school. But my father was perhaps an experimental hostage to be sent north, after an abysmal start in something known as an academy in Charleston. Older students told him he was supposed to purchase the steam radiator in his room. He used to say he ranked next to the top in his class at Hotchkiss—"we stood in a circle." He was old for his assigned class, took six years to get through the four years of Hotchkiss, and to be on the safe side about me, he entered me for a class four years later from the one from which I graduated.

The school was located in the northwest corner of Connecticut, Litchfield County, with the towns of Lime Rock, Sharon, Salisbury, and what do you know—Lakeville, site of Hotchkiss,

14

on Lake Wononscopomuc, near Twin Lakes, Bingham Pond, and Falls Village on the Housatonic. The area was at the tailing off of the Berkshires, where there were once located iron ore, forges, and foundries. I need only name the odd topics into which I could divert here—trout fishing, ice houses and ice-boating, canoeing, hiking, and the importance of making of Revolutionary-era cannon balls and chains. The closest rail station was Millerton, New York, after Millerites who feared, or hoped, that the world would come to an end at a date in the 1830s. I shall divert no further, but just say that the towns, the lakes, and the hills near Hotchkiss could make young boys conscious of their geography and history.

There are many influences, events, persons that either develop or inhibit a teenager. I went to this school because my father had gone there. It was the time of the Great Depression, and although I could not measure costs nor judge what was special, I did realize that my father suffered, in a relative sense, throughout my schoolboy years. Not that these rumors of suicides by brokers or selling apples by ordinary men were applicable to our step on the ladder. My father was gruff, but this seemed to hurt my sisters more than me. I had been conditioned for Hotchkiss by attendance at that New Hampshire camp. So at my new boarding school, I prospered at first. Low points, homesickness, only came in mid-winter after Christmas vacation. And when we rolled into spring my class in English got the shock of our young lives. We were berated, scolded, for the full fifty-minute period for our ineptitude and lack of effort. "Don't you realize how fortunate you are, what others are sacrificing for you?" The result was that we were deprived of three days of spring vacation, for mind-boggling, special tutoring. Disappointing one's parents was the given reason to heat up the steam of better academic achievement.

A more pleasant encouragement to learning stemmed from our Headmaster himself. We understood that he had been wounded in British service in WW I, and whether this was true or not, we noted that his handshake was flabby. He had greatness as a teacher and a leader that I much later personally experienced in Lord Louis, Admiral Mountbatten, and the best of Marine Corps officers. The man who is truly great will look a little boy, or subordinate, in the eye, listen to him, import something of importance or interest, and extract a response somehow that is expanding, rewarding to that lesser one, far beneath him. The Duke taught Bible, but I got nothing spiritual out of that. He instructed on being alert by showing how a puppy laps out of his water bowl, as opposed to the wise soldier dipping his hand into the stream, all the while looking right and left in awareness of where one was or danger threatened. This, I believe today, was a dramatization of the Wise and Foolish Virgins. Lord Louis looked me in the eye, gave me rapt attention at a busy, serious moment, and made sure I received a very personal note afterwards—all for a very minor occurrence in his life.

The Hotchkiss Athletic Director (still there from my father's time) was a coach of all the sports he could survey. I recall that he said if one could touch a thrown football, he should catch it. He pushed the out-of-doors, and there were directed walks in the winter woods, if you were not good enough for hockey. But I'll not forgive him for one decision. When it came time that the school could build a much needed new gym, reminding that this was the time of emergence from the Depression, he decreed that the gym be built with an ordinary, low ceiling. Forget about basketball.

We were subjected to a pretty rigorous academic trip. One imprecation, which might be called silly, unintelligible, or perhaps it was meant to be inspirational, was inscribed in bold letters about the rounded, open, ceiling space where we went to get to our mail boxes. It read, "I sat obedient, in the fiery prime of youth, self-governed at the foot of law." It was wasted on us teenagers, but it is remembered. All the Duke's luncheon or dinner table, we all had to take our turn at sitting next to him. At the time there was a popular movie playing with Fred Astaire and Ginger Rogers. It was about "Flying Down to Rio" where one might observe "An

Armadillo Dillowing in Its Armor." "What does that mean, Carrington? Explain how an armadillo might dillow in its armor." Well, I would attempt to mumble some sort of answer, but—! A better, more pleasant exclamation I heard in those times, but away from school, from Broadway. This occurred in the ditty "Wintergreen For President." It was a joyous, "Whatever It Is, I'm Against It!" The phrase is useful fun, allows one to be perverse, even sometimes treating apparent problems as solutions in disguise.

We got underway in French, Math, and the other subjects, but what I remember most dramatically was the study of Latin. First year there was Caesar and his Gallic Wars, O.K., but next came Cicero and Ovid, a perfect morass of the incomprehensible. I quit Latin, but resumed with Virgil in senior year. Rather fun. I tuned out on science in general after viewing a film about an operation in the extra-curricular Science Club. It made me queasy. Physics was most interesting, but how simple it was then, compared to what is being taught today! We had a history class conducted by a stutterer that was so boring, that he had us all watching the clock for the fifty-minute period to be up. Another class was conducted in three different sections. One test was repeated in each section, so when the third section did not perform well, the master chided us for not studying up on what we could know the earlier sections had caught. However, next time he gave three differing tests, so could say, "What did you expect, that I would give the same one again?" Of course, it was a stunt; just to make sure all were prepared for everything every time.

We got demerits or brownies for misdeeds, being tardy, or breaking minor rules. When an appearance was required, perhaps to offer an excuse, we could remember, "Very well, but do better next time." However, most impressive was the No Smoking edict. One year a group of seniors challenged this and were dismissed from the school. The lesson here was vastly greater than about tobacco: they were dismissed because they had broken their word of honor.

I cannot leave Hotchkiss on such a negative note. Almost all of us, although there were exceptions, experienced an abiding, extraordinary sense of camaraderie. Reunions are important. We encounter each other and the years roll away. We see each other again and feel it was just yesterday that we were together.

*   *   *

A hint of things to come in my future showed up after a visit of naval officers to Hotchkiss School, suggesting or offering the opportunity, but not recruiting, as is the expression today—for the Naval Reserve Officers Training Corps. It appealed to me for it seemed to be related to ships, the ocean, boats, and adventure. The army made no corresponding visiting pitch for a parallel ROTC program of training at my next level, Yale. I was to joke in later years, "I wanted to learn how to navigate my own yacht when I should have my yacht."

Upon embarkation on or into this interesting and tempting course or voyage, I was conscious of the events of the day, the international scene. Adolf Hitler was emerging in Germany, and the Japs were showing their muscle in Manchuria and North China. I cannot say that this was a true motive for signing up, but we, several like me at Hotchkiss, perhaps other "preppies" at other schools, declared our intent to try the naval service and adventure beyond our shores.

Arriving at college, what is remembered best today is not the uniforms, the drill, gunnery, navigation, or familiarity with the U.S. Navy. My strongest memory is of the character, leadership, cheerfulness, encouragement, and interest displayed in us by four chief petty officers who were at the source of our indoctrination and training as future officers. They all had short, Anglo names like Allen, Hook, or Jones. They all displayed impressive hash marks for multiple four-year hitches of service. Of the four, three showed solid gold, whilst one only flew his in red—let us believe that this was to indicate his specialization in engineering, though it might have meant something different.

I must interject what I heard many years later from a very senior admiral who had been superintendent of the Naval Academy. He related that there had been conducted a study of just which midshipmen turned out to be above the rest, who had attained highest rank. They looked at the scholars, those who had done best academically. No pattern there. They looked at the athletes. Again no evidence that early prowess might lead to future promotions. Rather, it turned out that those who had stuck their necks out, challenged authority or dogma in their way, who perhaps had a few demerits, even made some mistakes in their Annapolis lives—showed a pattern of becoming future leaders and attaining highest promotions. Take a look at what a great naval aviator, heroically surviving P.O.W. in North Vietnam, Sen. John McCain, has to say about his naughty midshipman days.

Academically we were required to undertake a course termed Classical Civilization. This replaced an old requirement for more Latin or Greek. That day was passing, for goodness sake, and I suppose Classical Civilization was valued as something that might begin to civilize us.

Another requirement was credit for three years of a foreign language. There was not the wide choice of languages that are offered today, and I chose French, having already had a good start. (Since I got on pretty well in Chinese later in my career and have sort of picked up Spanish in retirement as a Californian, there must have been some affinity for language there.) My sister has been an accomplished musician, and Chinese is certainly easier to get into for one with a musical ear. Economics was a total disaster, boring and incomprehensible. I guess I did not try.

One had choices among the science courses, and I ended up in Chemistry without participation in the laboratory and without enthusiasm. I have subsequently conjectured, were it possible, that Geology, Zoology, Astronomy, or Archaelogy would have fit me better.

What I ended up with were the Humane Letters. English History, English Constitutional History, French History, German History, plus a little exposure to Latin America and International Relations. Was this the ordinary path to becoming a regular Marine? However, there were also several courses in Literature, choices that eventually were more helpful in leading to that escape from captivity, the Marine Corps. It seems a stretch, but at the 50th Reunion of Iwo Jima, the secretary of the navy put a thrill into my spine when, bridging the chasms of time and even enmity, quoted Shakespeare's *Henry the Fifth,* "We few, we happy few, we band of brothers, For he today that sheds his blood with me, Shall be my brother. . . ."

Math was pretty advanced into "the" calculus. I did pretty well here, but then and to this day I cannot understand the "why" or "so what" in this discipline. It challenged us as a complicated stunt, but what were we being prepared to do, to calculate? Why was it "the?" A contrasting puzzle arose when the phrase "a" binomial system cropped up. "A" offers choice, but how can there but be one binominal system if the only, single, offering is yes or no, the light on or off, the way plus or minus? How can there be more than one binomial system? Too, we sometimes hear of something being "very" unique. If it is unique, one of a kind, it cannot be "very" (more, or less) other than uniquely itself. In this vein of inquiry, or thought, let us think of another brarnch of mathematics termed "loci." Don't linger long here, but know that the simplest definition offered by Webster's Dictionary is "the set of all points whose position is determined by stated conditions." Oh, well—let me leave this enthusiasm to later consideration of artillery high-angle fire in the campaign for Bougainville. And map correcting and surveying, in the assault and capture of Guam. And the differences and importance between rifled guns, and howitzers, and mortars in the battle and conquest of Iwo Jima.

There were slight, well, habits, at Yale that were not truly democratic. Yale tried to minimize the fraternity system by requiring all to live and feed in residential colleges, putting a bit of pressure on the old clubs. We did not have rooms therein, and any dining was a duplication and expense to parents for the meals taken. How could fraternities mesh with granting scholarships to the needy? In mine, in which I did not actively seek membership, "they" sought me out, not the other way around. A condition I exacted was that a couple of my close friends also be included. Too, I noted that, when it came time to select five fraternity officers from our class, a banding together in a voting decision to put their guys in the offices was organized by a group—from, whatta you know, a fraternity group still together from their preparatory school. With respect to Yale's secret senior societies I state they are none of my business, but they are surely undemocratic. This is the memoir of a Marine who learned never ask a man to do a job that he is not willing to do himself.

In the realm of fun and games, I loved baseball best. Perhaps it was because my Pops, although he was no athlete, still had played catch with me. The game caught my attention when fabled John McGraw was replaced on the New York Giants by Bill Terry. I was not skilled at baseball, so I competed for the position of manager. (Did not make it, but it was fun trying.) Our coach was Smokey Joe Wood, a 30-game winner of the distant past. A most memorable game was at Columbia from where, as every fan knows, emerged Lou Gehrig.

I had first been introduced to boxing at that summer camp in New Hampshire, and had continued fitfully at Hotchkiss School. I ceertainly was never a tough guy, or a pugilist, but I now gave it a try. Freshman year we would walk through the grubby New Haven streets to the Sterling Gymnasium, which had something of the appearance of a large church or cathedral. Wrestling was high up on an elevator trip, but at the very top floor we put on the gloves. There was much skipping rope, the light and the heavy punching bags, but we eventually got in the ring. It was mostly intramural stuff, for most colleges had by then given up the sport. I worried more than I should have about my endurance rather than getting after an opponent. There was satisfaction and reward in boxing. And, there was one real test. I recall one threatening, older, apparently tough and talented pug, who flexed his muscles and was something to admire on the heavy punching bag. I commented on him to our coach, an old pro named Mose King, whose reply was, "Yes, but he never gets in the ring." I drop another name with regard to boxing, adding to that of President-to-be Gerry Ford, with whom I sparred and who had escorted us into that memorable venture into the dominating atmosphere of West Point. Jack Dempsey was in the ring, as the third man, the referee, at the Yale Club in New York when our squad put on some exhibition matches.

Years later, in New Zealand and on Guadalcanal, my survey sergeant fancied himself a bit of a fighter. His interest in the sport and my help led to a loosely organized 12th Marine Regiment boxing team. On Guam, the team sought competition, but the only opposition that might be scheduled was a team from a Marine Corps ammunition company. It was an organization of blacks, and at the time the Marine Corps had not yet integrated that minority into regular line units of a division. Our regimental commander, probably a Southerner, forbad the matches. I guess one should not fault his decision. It was a measure of the times, in which the naval service lagged behind.

I am trying to graduate from these bright, college years, having opened with a tribute to NROTC and those four impressive chief petty officers who so contributed to our development of character. At conclusion of freshman year we could sign up for a cruise on the battleship *Wyoming,* scheduled to take us and those from NROTC units at other colleges to Havana and Guantanamo. We got underway from New Haven in very unimpressive fashion on board an ancient Eagle Boat for the shuttle down to Staten Island. A couple of items of naval indoctrination must be introduced. On the way through the East River and the dirty waters between Manhattan and Brooklyn, rough old sailors teasing us college boys, would point to white, rubbery, little bags floating alongside with, "See them little things? They're called Coney Island White Fish." On board the *Wyoming* there were lots of new sights and sounds. A sight was the tattoos of many of those pre-war tars. Perhaps they were the sorts that would boast toughness, adventure, even a thumbing of the nose at outsiders. I have an antipathy to this day about tattoos. One buttocks display read, "Twin Screws, Stand Clear." That is not hard to picture? And a blaring announcement, "Now hear this. All men receiving Salvarsan report to the sickbay immediately." Know what that meant?

On the run south to Cuba we got a taste of serious stuff, gunnery training on the 5-inch rifles. I term them thus for they indeed were rifles and were not to be confused with guns. The target was a curtain on a barge towed by a tug at some thousands of yards parallel to our course. The noise of firing was something that made you put in your earplugs. We learned how to ram a shell into the breech, followed by powder bags. We performed at the duties of pointer and trainer. Memory also includes the importance of wiping or swabbing the reopened pad of the breech just in case sparks might remain. We were coached, too, on what was known as hangfire, when the round for some reason did not go off. If one should belatedly go off, especially inside a turret, there is catastrophe. Why fuss about "rifles," instead of "guns?" In Marine Corps boot camp a recruit is taught the difference betwen a rifle, his very essence, soul, or reason for being as distinguished from something called a "gun." A boot, committing the gaffe of calling his weapon a gun, was required to parade, naked, his weapon at Port Arms, declaiming "This is my rifle, this is my gun; this is for fighting, this is for fun."

Havana was an exciting stop. When we arrived who should be first up the gangway but one of our own, Ernie, whose father had known many of ours and who himself was our classmate, home for summer vacation. To tease him we called him "our little brown brother," after President McKinley's bust. Ernie gave us a wonderful time—visiting Sloppy Joe's Bar, the Havana Yacht Club, even watching polo at the Havana Country Club. One evening he took us to the Copacabana, an elegant nightclub, with dates from the finest, along with their duennas just to make sure of our behaivor. A couple of our band in just a few days became so enamored with these new ladies that we joked about being certain that they then and there did not jump ship. Another evening, not quite so elegant, had us being entertained at "Shoeing the Mule," a very lively dance, at a very contrasting venue.

Along with this lively nightlife, however, the show went on. Reveille was very early, and we learned what holystoning the wooden decks meant. It was quite a drill, very tedious, to learn how to bundle up our hammocks, which we slung on the gun deck, to stumble down ladders, not stairs, to a storage area for them. Some hot nights it was easier to sleep on a crooked arm right on the softer wooden deck or a harder slab of the steel nearby. I was assigned a daily cleaning station with another pal, high up above everything. (It might have been called the crosstree on a sailing craft.) One day, exhausted from Havana nightlife, we decided that we would escape duty and observation. It was a good spot in which to take a big sleep. Our most respected Chief Petty Officer Allen caught us. We got the most severe "reading off" of our young lives. I never received a scolding or berating to match his for the rest of my life. It was something like, "Don't you know there is a war coming? How dare you little bums think you can get away with this! Don't you know how lucky, how privileged, you are? Next time I'll have you keel hauled!" That last part was truly not feasible, but we caught his meaning.

At Guantanamo, which our nation would come to utilize as an incarceration spot for the motley collection rounded up in Afghanistan, our primary activity was softball on the flat, sandy plane. We were prohibited from wandering into the dirty little town of Cabanera. I was to experience Guantanamo yet again a couple of more times in my life. I visited there from Puerto Rico on a New Year's Day in the Fidel Castro era with the chairman of the Joint Chiefs of Staff, Gen. Maxwell Taylor, to whom I was an aide. He wanted to know first-hand about this potential hot spot. Finally one Halloween in retirement I encountered Jack Nicholson, movie star, who greeted me out of the darkness. "I hear you were in the Marine Corps. I'm making a movie called *A Few Good Men.*" It was a tale about Guantanamo, and I tried to hit him up thereafter for my favorite charity, the Marine Military Academy. No luck.

*   *   *

The summer of 1940 I climbed with a pal to the summit of Mt. Katahdin, begining of the Appalachian Trail "down" in Maine, as they say. Why "down?" Because in colonial times it was the homeward way, down to Europe. Close by, at next stop, was the St. Lawrence waterway, start of the difficult path for ships assembling in convoy to save Europe from Hitler. We circled the Gaspé Peninsula, of a Canada then at war, viewing the rugged little trawlers or cargo vessels assembling in the broad mouth of the St. Lawrence. Heavy cement covered all the pilot houses with only slits to see ahead, for air attack and the other threat, submarines. We circled the Gaspé counterclockwise, keeping to the right on a rather narrow little motorway, despite our mommas' directions to do it clockwise so we would not accidentally tumble into the Atlantic.

And elsewhere that summer in small boat in Vineyard Sound, between Hyannis—you have heard of it—and Martha's Vineyard, we observed a new type of very fast motorboat, maneuvering excitedly and throwing up big tail spray. Could it have been JFK getting trained or conducting training for his PT boat future in the South Pacific?

My father, a WW I naval officer, got us ceremonial invitations to observe the launching of a new cruiser, as President Roosevelt readied the nation for war. Secretary of the Navy James Forestall presided as Margaret Mitchell, authoress of *Gone with the Wind,* smashed the champagne bottle, crying out, "Ah crissen thee Atlanta!"

After the Cuban days, a couple of years later in the summer of 1941 and the war having already started and England in a desperate situation up against German submarine warfare, we embarked on our final NROTC cruise on a converted yacht. We merely adventured about Long Island Sound, a pleasant little ocean for us. We called at a yacht club on Long Island, where one of our guys was a member, we made the Yale–Harvard boat races in New London, where we were able to look up girlfriends at Connecticut College for Women. The *Sylph* rolled so much when we rounded the tip of Long Island that we scurried back into calmer waters. The cream of the navy was being lined up to help Britain engage the Germans in sub warfare near Iceland or to escort convoys out of Canadian waters to Britain. The captain surely was no less than a counterpart of Captain Queeg of *Caine Mutiny Court Martial* fame, and the crew was surly and complaining. Perhaps at this time I began thinking about other alternatives to this branch of the naval service, or wondering how my classmates in the U.S. Army, ROTC unit were making out.

Childhood and Training

Battleship *Wyoming*, Havana, Cuba, 1939

***Sylph*, New York, 1941**

NROTC Gets Ready For War

75-mm Howitzers

Whangarei, New Zealand

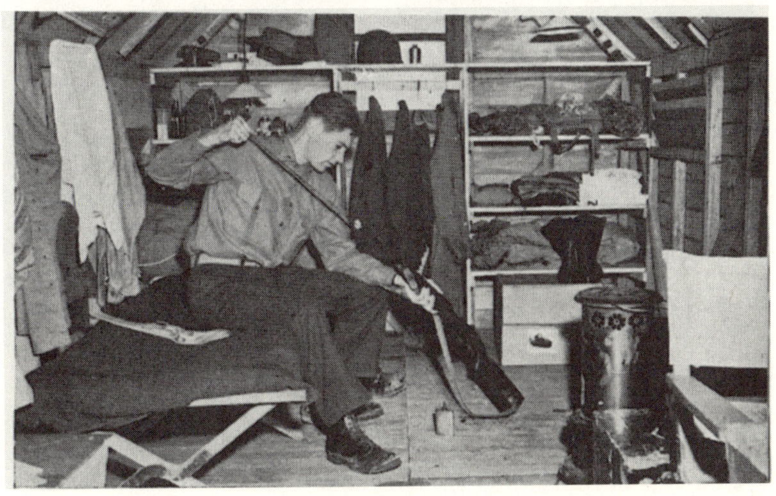

How We Lived, New Zealand

How We Looked, Guadalcanal

THREE

Reserve Officers' Course, Quantico; and Imperial Valley, California

A loosening of my shackles took place in the spring of 1941, after Pearl Harbor, when the movie actor John Payne played in *Shores of Tripoli,* a movie shown then in New Haven. It could not truly have been about 19th Century Barbary pirates, but certainly it glorified the United States Marine Corps. It inspired inquiry into this other part of the naval service and led to the revelation that a NROTC grad could get in as a 2nd Lt., USMCR.

A first worry was a uniform. What might tailors know about USMC uniforms, Sam Browne belts, proper shoes and socks? Many of my classmates could wear their new naval uniforms at graduation, but I had to negotiate a little blindly for the new costume in New York City. Soon, however, one could finish up this detail in Quantico at Al Bologna's (known as Al Baloney-Nose's). On the way I was sworn in as a 2nd Lt. at the Broadway recruiting office by a gruff veteran, recalled-to-active-duty, major who tried to frighten me on what tremendous challenges and problems lay ahead. Maybe so, but indeed I was to experience much more combat and many more adventures than he.

I was physically well-fit, though much younger and more naive than plenty of my fellow arriving classmates for the 9th Reserve Officers' Training Course. A USN doctor, old-timer, seemed delighted to jokingly inquire not "if" you had ever had, but "when was the last time you had a venereal disease?" Early on we were tutored or reminded that Marines render and return salutes and with dignity overtake a superior with a mannerly, "By your leave, sir." We do not keep our hats on in the mess hall, put our hands in our pockets, carry such ignominious items as umbrellas, and salute when uncovered. A contrasting precept learned in the classroom was R.H.I.P., standing for "Rank Has Its Privileges," delivered by a rather stuffy, overweight senior, which lesson fell pretty flat at the time. More importantly were heard and always remembered, "Never ask a man to do a job that you are unwilling to do yourself" and in a combat situation, "Officers eat at the end of the chow line." My first night in barracks I ignorantly donned pajamas, and was laughed at. Never again! Skivvy shirts and drawers were of course the way to go. This brings to mind another teaching, "Women wear pants, Marines wear trousers."

There was a competitive atmosphere at Quantico. After morning formation we would be dismissed. With only a short time to get shaved and with fewer wash basins than there were guys trying to get to them, I quickly learned how to stand in a rear rank, jump over a small hedge, and get up the stairs in time. Another contrasting lesson was that one helps a buddy. I did not know much about making up my bunk, to the degree that one could bounce a dime off it, so I was lucky enough to be helped by a seasoned ex-sergeant who knew all the ropes. Years later I observed a field training exercise from a hilltop, watching recruits toil up the hill. The smallest, weakest youngster was deliberately saddled with the heavy load, perhaps the baseplate of a heavy mortar, close by another, well-built, powerful, athletic recruit. The seasoned training officer in charge told me just to watch. Soon indeed the bigger guy helped his struggling buddy. Their loads were swapped, and voluntarily.

I then did not know beans about rifles and pistols—how to take them apart, how to clean them, how to inspect them, and how seriously to fire them. A Colt .45 pistol became my combat and ceremonial weapon, and over the years I taught myself about it. As a major on duty at Headquarters Marine Corps, with WW II on the islands of the Pacific, training in the Chinese language, and subsequent Chinese service under my belt (but never having had the opportunity in such assignments for qualification on the rifle range, and with Korean combat and command coming up) I felt deprived, inadequate, and overlooked. I went out of my way with a reluctant senior to set up a daily 4:00 A.M. reveille at my Fairfax home, to arrive at Quantico before dawn to participate without insignia of rank with the enlisted men, firing for qualification on the rifle range, and still make the boring duties at HQMC. A few years and many adventures later I felt pride in leading Second Marine Division battalion competition for highest qualification percentage of Marines within the command, with not one but two, separate, artillery battalions over two, successive years.

*　　*　　*

After our 1942, 9th ROC, basic infantry indoctrination there came training as an artillery officer. Yes, I suppose it was mathematics in my background of schooling, but the comment is that we in those days were so motivated that we were very disappointed when we were not directed into infantry. In the end, however, field artillery could be regarded as the fraternity within the fraternity. The basic weapon then was the 75-millimeter, pack howitzer. It was Model 98, meaning designed in 1898, and "pack" signified that it was to be broken down in parts, loaded on the pack-animal horse or mule, for transport for frontline support. One fallout from this was that we were trained in Equitation! This was conducted on large horses—could they have been only available because of polo, still then played at Quantico? True cavalry was disappearing onto motorcycles, and the few horses still available to the U.S. Army were for funeral duty at nearby Fort Meyer.

Two episodes reside in memory when we galloped about the Quantico woods, perhaps abreast on narrow trails and trying to not

33

lose our pith helmets, desperate not to topple off out of the saddle. Our very severe instructor would bellow, "Lieutenant, who gave you permission to dismount?" and then to others who were entertained, "Who gave you permission to laugh?" I cannot leave the subject of horses and mules without recalling a Guadalcanal moment. The command was sore put for supplies and reinforcements, and shipping was limited. Some planners, knowing that Marine Corps artillery was equipped with 75-mm pack howitzers, which were by then indeed trundled about in jeeps or trucks, loaded a whole ship with nothing but hay or feed for our assumed steeds. Marines had to unload this in night working parties, for no real purpose.

At Marine Corps Schools, Quantico, we learned new skills, concepts, and terminology, in the classroom and in the field. There were simple precepts, such as seizing the high ground and holding it, how to plan night defensive lines of fire, what was meant by the military crest of a hill, duties on a patrol of the point and flankers, and always having a reserve element. We were readied for leadership at the platoon or company level. The big Marine Corps itself was pioneering in the field of amphibious warfare—but this was yet to come for us.

For one interested in geography and history, Quantico was a great scene. It was on the R.F.&P. (yes, the Richmond, Fredericksburg and Potomac Railroad. Richmond, the last stand for Robert E. Lee, and Fredericksburg, where Lincoln had another of his misfortunes in finding a general). So we students enjoyed and profited by excursions to visit there and at other Civil War battlefields, nearby Bull Run and more distant Gettysburg. On a later tour at Marine Corps Schools I was to commute south from Fairfax Courthouse, as it was called, down through Annasquam, once a minor Potomac port. Then at the end of the day I would reverse course, back through home in Fairfax, then on past Robert Kennedy's Hickory Hill, over the Chain Bridge, and up Reno Road to American University.

*   *   *

For there to be progress in my career I next had to weigh anchor, to move along out of Marine Corps Schools, Quantico. How much indeed did that anchor weigh? I had to get underway, even if my ship's way on was just within the United States. Check up in Webster's if you think this mariner is confused or has misspelled "weigh" and "way."

Off for California went the vast majority of the 9th ROC. It was the way to the Pacific, and the direction of our business with Japan. Guadalcanal was grabbing the headlines, but other Marines, recruits from our two Recruit Training Commands, Parris Island and San Diego; old timers getting reassigned from many spots, including Iceland; and new officers, as we, were headed for the Third Marine Division, getting put together primarily at Camp Pendleton, California. America's capability to move large loads of personnel by air was beginning to flourish, so after five days of travel allowance at home, I was able to get aboard, New York to Los Angeles. At one stop some passengers were bumped, for it was the site of new aircraft construction and priority had to be granted to busy ferry pilots, picking up new aircraft. This fresh, young, new lieutenant remembers retaining his seat, personally surrendered up by a real Auntie Mame, a showgirl perhaps, but certainly a patriot ceding position to a very minor cog in the machine.

I first set foot in California, at Burbank air terminal. The delicious continuation of this arrival is that today I reside close to Burbank airport. The central tower, heart of the terminal, looks exactly today as it did sixty years ago. Bus to Los Angeles Union Rail Station, and it, too, appears unchanged. Destination was Oceanside, and it is my recollection that we were issued weapons and put on trucks in the middle of that very night for our field artillery futures in the 12th Regiment. Third Marine Division. None of our small group, primarily easterners, had the slightest knowledge of Camp Dunlop, Niland, Calipatria, Brawley, El Centro, and Calexico—locals in the Imperial Valley. This area was tenderly irrigated by the All-American Canal, but, to be sure, adjoined to real desert and mountains, ideal for us to get used to tents, jeeps, FWDs or four-wheel trucks, radios and field telephones, mess halls, the brig, and our howitzers. We had advanced beyond Quantico.

Our troops were building up, but few were experienced. It was noticeable that there was only a framework of officers in my assigned 4th Battalion, but several more were to arrive from the Army's Fort Sill and more advanced training than my gang. Marine divisions were triangular in organization—that is to say, the three infantry regiments were directly supported by three artillery battalions. But my 105-mm howitzer battalion was to operate a bit separately in general support of the entire division. In our busy training at artillery support, the open desert streamed away interminably from Camp Dunlop, to the degree that it was difficult to estimate range with the eye. Too, there were few distinguishable landmarks to select as targets. "See that bushy bush?" could not be very precise. As a result considerable effort was one day put into acquiring some old, wooden privies and transporting them laboriously into the target area so we'd have something to shoot at. George Carrington early on, registering with only single rounds from one section of his four-howitzer battery, hit that privy square on. It vanished completely. I guess I acquired an aura of luck, if not competency, when I next could order "Fire For Effect." Training is a boring business so not much need be remembered, but this. One night riding in a jeep our two-star major general, the very division commander, tried a test of morale or a venture at familiarity, asking his driver "How do you like the Marine Corps, son?" Answer: "Not worth a shit, Mac, how about you?" Well, there was more of discipline, of training, and of trial, ahead for all of us.

On the matter of discipline my battalion was to be wonderfully free of misbehavior, need for courts-martial, in our time in

World War II. Let it be credited to our leader, Lt. Col. Hope Kirk, of whom more later. At Camp Dunlop he took a look at one of his lieutenants John Jaqua who had been editor of the Yale Law Review, the most prestigious achievement at that pretty good university. He made him prosecutor for any courts-martial, and added that this here George Carrington will be defense counsel. I do not now record any great skirmishes against each other, but this. On one occasion we experienced what was known as Command Influence, the big regimental colonel or Convening Authority interfering to tell us what he wanted the court's finding to be. This was once-upon-a-time-long-ago stuff to us blazing, idealistic, college graduate, new Marine Corps guys. I don't know that we said it, but our attitude was "forget it."

*　　*　　*

At this Camp Dunlop, Niland, California scene where I found myself in 1942, the subject of the geography intensely interested me. I have to know where the rivers are flowing and to what destinations do the highways and roads connect. Here in the southwest corner of our country were the Chocolate Mountains, the Colorado River, and the Salton Sea. We once were allowed a special weekend of liberty in fabled Los Angeles, Hollywood, an anticipated heaven itself. The Southern Pacific running through Niland picked us up, but further along the way there occurred a washout on the tracks. Never mind, one of us who was a lieutenant from UCLA, took over. "There is a stop we can make at Indio, and there is a great place called Palm Springs nearby." We had that heavenly weekend after all. And also nearby was the Salton Sea, below sea level. There had been built up over eons of time a deep sill of mud blocking it from the Gulf of California. I was fascinated to read once of the theory that, given just the right combination of tides, storms, and winds—the Gulf waters could rise up and inundate that mud sill and again connect to the Salton.

37

Let me relate how I was to get underway when this California, Imperial Valley, Camp Dunlop interval should come to a close. We had to transit the mountain range, hauling our gear for combat and towing our 105s, to the Recruit Depot San Diego over the worst, most hazardous road of all time. The Yuma to San Diego railroad had to divert for a stretch into Mexico, due to the tortuous path here. It was a geographical curiosity interesting for me. That transfer was marked by an accident that shocked us neophytes. One of our howitzer sections, the FWD truck, all crew members, their gear, and the towed weapon, did not make one turn or descent and tumbled into a precipitous canyon.

Before departing San Diego I made first lieutenant, being surprised at the short time for this award since I had embarked on the journey. The pressure or necessity for more officers and men was building up, so promote them to make more room at the bottom. We boarded a South African merchant vessel with destination New Zealand. Say it like a seaman—in *Bloemfontaine,* by Cook Island, for Auckland—not on some ship, through or via, to somewhere.

FOUR

Training in New Zealand and on Guadalcanal

En route to New Zealand the ship was good enough, but far from a regular USN troop transport. Men bunked in altered cargo holds and often stood in line continuously, waiting for one meal and then wanting to get to the head of chow line for the next. The voyage was easy. There truly were no Jap submarines that might wander into this part of the Pacific, although we were fervently warned of their possible presence. A Marine once carelessly tossed a couple of orange rinds overboard. Some overzealous disciplinarian was all for court-martial, but a more mature decision was of course reached. I do recall one episode at sea on a transport, at a bit later time, to which I admit my only WW II sensation of fear. This was a clanging alarm of fire at night. *"All Hands Man Your Embarkation Stations!"* It was false, but was a situation in which embarked Marines could do nothing; only feel helpless, out of their element.

It was a bit of a shock to discover New Zealander dockworkers were on strike, and on another occasion to find that in this fair land even in wartime everything stops for extended tea-time. I have to include, though, that New Zealanders and Australians had sacrificed gallantly, the Anzac forces being withheld from return home by Winston Churchill in the critical necessity of slowing the German timetable, if not completely stopping them. There was then too a scarcity in homeland manpower and with the

Japs threatening in New Guinea, we arriving Marines were greeted as heroes, admittedly before the fact.

We headed for camp in the north end of the North Island. Here we were billeted in 6- or 8-man huts near the pleasant town of Whangarei, near the Bay of Islands. More field firing exercises over a range from which the sheep had been evicted. In that land it seemed odd for a Yank to overhear a New Zealander contemplating his first choice on a menu, "I believe I'll have a nice slice of mutton." Driving in our jeep one day my city-boy driver who alleged great knowledge and familiarity with cities and countryside, persons and animals, spotted some sheep, but gave something away by his "Hey, what are them things? I never seen nuttin' like that." And once during firing exercises at an extreme range there extended a minor telephone line, running on skinny poles with perhaps only one strand. It seemed incredible that a 105-round could hit and break it, but so it did, leading to apologetic renegotiation of our privilege of training there.

Artillerymen usually got to ride in trucks and jeeps, but certainly there was a requirement that we be as physically fit as those who had nothing but their own legs to propel them. This makes me interject that in our operations a Marine infantry battalion then had only two jeeps, making it very tough to evacuate the wounded. Hence, stretcher-bearers, including bandsmen not at the time needed for music or parades. Resuming, all personnel of the Third Marine Division were required to complete 60-mile hikes. Conveniently for my 4/12 unit we were at one end of a 30-mile track between east and west shores bordering the peninsula which formed New Zealand's northern tip. This made for an interesting stroll and an overnight bivouac within joined shelter-halves one night for me and Jim Garnett, another first lieutenant pal. He would claim that I kicked apart said tent in the rainy night to the result that he came up later with a mild case of pleurisy. That put him in the Whangarei infirmary, where he was attended not by nurses but by "sisters." I had an interesting encounter on my very last night in

Auckland. Guadalcanal was to be next. We Marines on a last night of liberty in civilized surroundings found ourselves at a farewell party in company with members of the Yale University Naval Medical Unit. I ran into the very doc who, not so long before, had ruled that I did not really need a knee operation, maybe from skiing or soccer that would have prevented me from a commission in the Marine Corps. In short, his decision enabled my chance at Guadalcanal. Sort of an entertaining surmise, not to be taken seriously. We were glad and eager for the next move.

Liberty was pretty good and very welcomed in Whangarei, but everything was puritanically closed down on Sundays. Some romantic liaisons cropped up, one impressive one being that of a Marine, who after a vigorous training day, would still hike the twelve miles into town just to see his gal, and return to his cot in his hut. We got to a few movies, where we found ourselves within the realm of the empire, standing respectfully at the start of a show to the music of "God Save The King." A rail journey on a narrow-gauge line, maybe more like a long trolley ride, got you to Auckland. My Yale *Law Review* editor buddy planned that we attend a meeting of the Supreme Court of New Zealand. I was intrigued to observe justices in wigs presiding over a murder trial for an incident on Norfolk Island. Norfolk had been an overflow, dumping ground for repeat offenders out of the numbers of supposed criminals, which England had traditionally banished to Australia. There was no such thing as a court of law, for such a crime, on Norfolk. Auckland was not exciting for hotshot Yanks. We were welcomed into homes, met some gals, observed that there were no extremes of poverty and affluence, sighted very few two-story homes, and couldn't be bothered with occasional horse races. New Zealand was an enjoyable capitalist society, but had a veneer of socialism. Goodbye Auckland. Hello Guadacanal.

*　*　*

That island had seen desperate combat, on land principally by the First Marine Division, and at sea by the U.S. Navy. We Third MarDiv elements were still getting organized, one regiment having been sitting in Fiji. Guadalcanal for us was more training, a few funny stories, and a siege of boredom. It was split in two parts, before and after the more serious stuff, shall we put it—commitment in November 1943 to the assault upon Bougainville.

Professionally (that is in matters of field artillery training), the 12th Regiment began to coordinate massed fires, moving weapons in the jungle, and honing gunnery and communications. 105 howitzers were usually loaded into a LST, hitched behind their trucks and pulled across the ramp and onto the beach. However, we also practiced the interesting option of putting the weapon into an amphibious truck, (DUKW), or "duck." It could not fit just right so had to be cocked in at an angle, to be lifted out by a crane and towed to where needed. I was to have the experience of both modes—by the beached ramp for Bougainville and by the "duck" for Guam. This just has now to be said, the images of amphibious craft or ships in mind. Marines were never happier than when they could get on that beach and go forward in their own element. And the navy and all sailors I am certain were never more relieved than when they could retract and get again to sea.

I was the survey officer for my battalion, not completely understanding the need for many and long surveying legs through jungle trails, when one could just stick guns and registration point on a map or chart and correct from there. Especially aggravating were the heat, mud, and entangling vines, which we called "Oh shit, vines." On my own I was intrigued to meet and experiment with the regimental survey officer, who operated a theodolite rather than a simple, battalion device called an aiming circle. This also led me to fiddle with rectifying or putting a grid on a aerial photo which was distorted for having been taken at an angle rather than directly overhead. And I had the initiative to suggest sighting or directing the aim of our artillery batteries by reliance on a distant aiming point, say a hillcrest or peak, rather than unstable, close-in aiming stakes. There was to come, probably out of this, a tremendous surprise and defining turn in my life. One day the dispatch came in to make the offer of a regular commission, USMC vice USMCR, to this young, callow lieutenant. I was inclined to decline it, maybe still dreaming about what—law school, or being a banker, or selling buggy whips? I dunno. But my commanding officer said, "Take it, George. You can still get out after the war if you want." So I did. Only one funny thing to add. After the war most got what was termed mustering-out pay. We fortunate few were never to be "out," so no $300.

On one of our first nights on Guadalcanal our small advance party was alerted by an air raid. Heck, it could have been fifty miles away, a single Jap night reconnaissance aircraft just looking around. This was nothing like earlier combat on Guadalcanal. Our excitable senior officer present decided that the thing to do was to call the roll. Where would anyone have gone from our spot in the coconut palm plantation where we were encamped? On other such interventions it was irritating that the movies had to be suspended. Movies were important. When they were interrupted all one could try and do was to pump up his Coleman lantern (a nuisance that was difficult to manage and which attracted mosquitoes) so one could try to read. In rainy season the slit trenches next to our tents were suggested as refuges, but who wanted to get out of a cot and into such a wet hole for such an unlikely threat? We regarded air raids by Japs with great scorn. When Marines were sometimes summoned to go out on night working parties to unload merchant ships, an air raid warning might be sounded. Maybe one occurred once or occasionally, but the rumor spread was that this was the time for the merchant ship, at anchor, to weigh that anchor, steam perhaps one hundred yards, re-anchor, and thus be able to claim underway pay or exposure to two raids vice one, meaning bonus pay for them, not us.

Leaving the realm of professionalism, training, the serious

stuff, there were entertaining, funny times on Guadalcanal. Once there was a reportedly very important inspection visit by Eleanor Roosevelt. Guadalcanal had a long, coastal expanse, the trail connecting all sorts of combat, supply, supporting or garrison installations, of Marines, Navy, Army, and Army Air Corps. There were no women in our midst, none except the occasionally glimpsed Solomon Islander. If anyone should touch one of them, we were threatened, you would catch the "awful-awful" and they would never let you go home. Such was not the lot with other Marines, in Australia, New Zealand or Hawaii—with all those gals we jealously thought. But when Eleanor visited, the order went out that for miles and miles all pee tubes had to be screened. She probably observed very little and certainly never came close to viewing the hundreds of stitched-together ammo containers, pee tubes, for the thousands of Guadalcanal guys.

My unit was located in a carefully planted coconut plantation, reportedly owned by the Lever Brothers firm, utilized for soap manufacture. You cannot destroy any of the palms, we were ordered, for then compensation had to be paid to those Levers. Some Marines experimentally had to emulate the natives' skill in climbing said palms. Inevitably there were ghastly broken leg accidents. The plantation was at some distance from the beach. That meant we had to be trucked some distance for swimming call, and it was a shame that when all returned they were inevitably covered with the dust of the earth. A rotated responsibility was that of a lieutenant selected daily to preside over the garbage scow, necessary to dump the tons of waste and trash from our polluted camps into the sea. The scow was called Chanel #5.

One must tell of our respected naval comrades and associates. Of course, all know of the importance of the faithful naval corpsmen in our ranks. Many Marines can recall that if or when we qualified for that Purple Heart, we treasured field care from an enlisted corpsman, over and beyond that from a nurse who might eventually reach us later in some hospital. Our officers included the chaplains, dentists, and doctors. I fear that the chaplain of the 12th Regiment did not get heavy attendance at Sunday services. In time of crisis there was not a "God Is My Co-Pilot" spirit among us. It was our spiritual inadequacy, not his. Our particular dentist was a jolly fellow. In this early time on Guadalcanal the trouble was that his drill had to be cradle-pumped by the patient himself during treatment, no electric power then available. Our spirited regimental doctor is fondly remembered. He boasted jokingly that his preferred food from the hunt was crocodile, not alligator. But best was his lecture to all hands, a warning against contracting dysentery, a crippling infirmity for a command. He warned of the extreme importance of keeping flies, carrying infection from what the naval service calls heads, to food. He called his lecture, "How To Make A Shit Sandwich."

World War II

Getting Ashore, Bougainville

The Mud Of Bougainville

All Depended On Communications

Getting Out Of An Amtrac, Guam

105-mm Howitzer, Guam

Awarded A Purple Heart

On The Beach, Iwo Jima

75-mm Pack Howitzer And Suribachi, Iwo Jima

FIVE

Combat on Bougainville, Guam, and Iwo Jima

The Third Marine Division saw its first action on Bougainville, a short step northwest of Guadalcanal and named after the French navigator who had accompanied Montcalm to Canada, established a colony on the Falklands, made a voyage around the world rediscovering the Solomon Islands, and fought Admiral Hood at Martinique. Pretty big doings, yet he is primarily remembered in the name of the lovely bougainvillea vine. Our step could be called short because still to come was the bypassing of many Jap holdings as America's sea power grew and dominated.

We landed at Empress Augusta Bay, mostly unopposed, but on a narrow beach that became littered with broached and broken landing craft, distant from the main Jap stronghold of Kieta. In pre-combat planning there had been the thought of emplacing artillery on a neat little islet, Puruata, just off the beachhead. That intention was junked when it was found that the undergrowth on Puruata was so dense that one could hardly reach the ground. So, on the beach we found suitable positions for most of our howitzers, but there was a complicating factor for at least some 12th Marines batteries.

The coconut palms were so dense and high that in some directions, or deflections as gunners would say, rounds might go off in the palm fronds right in front of us. That meant resort to high-angle fire. Pause to consider what this necessitated in order to mass si-

multaneous impact of battalion or regimental fire missions on targets. Firing tables had been designed by the army at Aberdeen
Proving Ground, Maryland, but who knew how old or inaccurate
these, or indeed our pre-used howitzer tubes, might be? There had
to be careful experimentation and use of a stopwatch. It does not
take much to grasp that there are appreciable differences in times
of flight between direct and high-angle firing. We also had at times
to try high-angle for short range missions, where range decreases
with higher settings. Nobody wanted to reach the point at which a
round might go so straight up that it could tumble back, too dan-
gerously close. Got the picture?

At the other end of matters, providing front-line support for
infantry in the jungle, artillery had other delicate responsibilities.
The new, proximity fuse was coming into use, so even if we had
the range down pretty well, don't let anything get too close, into
those trees or palms. And always, *always* be very sure that the correct number of ammunition bags get loaded. Almost enough of artillery, but there is one other achievement which has to be told. A
single Jap field piece at a pretty great but hard-to-figure range had
been dodging out of the jungle onto the beach and taking quick
shots at us before scurrying back into hiding. We could see the exact deflection, and I claim credit for suggesting that the known
speed of sound and the stopwatch be consulted. We sure finished
him.

A principal achievement of the artillery on Bougainville was
the battering given a trail junction, a Jap assembly area, termed
Piva Forks. Fire support and operational and intelligence information on front line situations was undependable by radio, so the important priority was to get telephone lines set up. The terrible mud
through which churned the amphibian tractors and trucks meant
constant struggle to keep those lines in. Not hard to imagine what
those amtracs and "ducks" did to wire. The wire crews had to labor
continuously, night and day, replacing broken lines and attempting to overhead them. At the battle for Piva Forks the sole line of

communications for the entire division, front back to rear, rested on that of the 4th Battalion. We had one by-the-book forward observer, my pal, Lt. Orrin Johnson, who so deliberately, calmly, and systematically went through the prescribed routine of a report, that the division commander himself had to intervene with his priorities.

An early shock occurred during a torrential rainstorm during our second or third night. A coconut palm came crashing down on our fire direction tent, hitting the operations officer square on top of his head. Assignments had to be altered, and I was found useful in the duties of fire direction, as well as those of survey officer. Someone also picked me for the job of malarial control officer. On Guadalcanal I was required to see that standing water surfaces where mosquitoes might breed were oiled over and that a defensive spraying of camp areas had to be conducted nightly. So, on Bougainville I was among the first to catch malaria. That resulted in a secondary learning lesson for me. Until I fully recovered, I was assigned to fill the not very demanding task of liaison to one of the infantry regiments. Malaria had laid low, for extended periods, many of our predecessors on Guadalcanal. Third Marine Division personnel had been ordered to start their atabrine pills well before arrival in the Solomons, and we seemed better protected. Why, then, was I the first to get it in my outfit? Anyway I was stuck in a large trench but beneath plenty of canvas, and I knew the corpsmen had plenty more serious business than mine to take care of. I recall being vague about passage of time. Was it day or night? When did you last talk to me? Perhaps I did not miss much nor was I missed importantly in my outfit. The bonus was, however, to participate in the headquarters of a gallant infantry regiment and to observe how professionally and calmly they directed their men.

We watched while engineers built a new airstrip, crushed coral being a great foundation for the runway. On one occasion a friendly (probably one of our own) Marine Corps aircraft, took a close-in course, swooping and banking to show his markings.

Green anti-aircraft crews, committed to combat for the first time, impulsively fired at him but luckily missed. There was little enemy air to threaten us—except for "Washing Machine Charlie," as a lone, night reconnaissance, Jap, aircraft might be called. There occurred a notable exception one evening as we reclined at night and heard an aircraft overhead. The thing automatically to say was. "That's one of ours!" It was not, and though only a single bomb landed a great distance from us, it had us scrambling for our slit trenches.

We had been exposed to Solomon Islands weather during our time on Guadalcanal. The rain would come down in torrents, usually in the late afternoon, and then clear up pretty rapidly. Bougainville, too, was one wet scene, and most troops only had shelter halves in which to settle down. Sometimes the muddy soil was so fluid that it was difficult to make tent pegs stick. Rifles had always to be protected from the rain and dirt. Although there was no threat of Japs nearby our rear area field artillery unit, it was ordered that all personnel carry their weapons at all times.

This gave advantage to officers and communicators, as I remember. Their pistols hung on cartridge belts, but the riflemen had to sling their weapons on their backs. At the same time they would have to struggle through the mess line, one hand holding the double-dish, hinged mess gear and the other balancing a canteen cup. Note, however, that in combat officers ate at the end of the chow line. The messmen seemed to go out of the way in slinging the portions all on top of the other, getting a kick out of teasing their fellow Marines. Those canteen cups held about five cup loads. One refill per meal, three meals a day, meant about thirty cups a day. And if one should miss for a spell, that meant one big coffee-deprivation headache.

Neither Marines nor Japs mixed it up much at night. The division expanded its perimeter, and we got ready to be relieved by a U.S. Army division. We had inflatable rubber mattresses on which to lie at night, but they were sort of a nuisance. I developed one stunt that served me well. I had what was known as a clothing roll, sort of a Val pack. It was convenient just to open it up, not bother with unloading the pockets, and smoothing it out to become a readily movable bed. Honestly, I do not recall others trying this ready-solution. For a time we found ourselves on some low hills, but not far from the beach. Earthquakes occurred occasionally throughout the South Pacific islands, and it was an extraordinary feeling to experience one at this slight altitude. The earth did not quake; rather, it seemed as if we were being rolled about like Jell-O in a dish. There was mud everywhere on Bougainville, even on the hilltops.

We got splendid support from our doctors. I recall that every field artillery battalion had one doctor, and the infantry had two. The corpsmen lived among us, same uniforms and most chose indeed to carry a weapon. I must add that the 12th Marines had a chaplain, of what faith is forgotten, but I remember feeling sorry for him. There was little attendance at his weekly services—maybe because we had as yet not faced real dangers or maybe because we were just too young or too shallow.

There are many ordinary guys in combat and a few heroes, mostly infantry. However, one must now and here include a couple of incidents about which Marines can be well, embarrassed. A very senior officer, remembered now as corpulent and affecting a swagger stick, was queried how long it might take for a certain bridge to be set up, his staff responsibility. He replied that it might take about two weeks, though I confess that such a long ago estimate might have become exaggerated. Wonderful Navy Seabees supporting us merely answered, "If you give us lights, by morning!" And another, holding pretty high rank, did not like the muddy morass, which messed up access to his royal tent. Water, drinking water, a most precious item, transported in most precious, 5-gallon water cans, was a big logistical necessity for all. When he ordered that the cans be filled with sand to provide stepping stones to his tent, well—the big general, the division commander, relieved him of command.

We college boys, field artillery, having had that heavier dose of math, knew our jobs and would not let anyone hurt our leader, Lt. Col. Hope Kirk. Neither would Hope let anyone else tell him how to command. Example: Once, earlier in New Zealand before this first combat exposure, a sergeant had misappropriated a truck or jeep and had had an accident. The colonel, at the regimental level above Hope, ordered him to court-martial the offender. Reply: "No, sir. And besides I ordered him to have that accident." Another one learned from Hope, excusing misconduct or a misdeed was, "Anyway, he was drunk and asleep at the time." The whole point was that he taught us to train and trust a subordinate. He had to replace you if you became a casualty. Do not micromanage.

We had a joyous time in our war, of course interrupted now and then by real combat. Never any problems with discipline. One could even say that the looser the control the better the performance. One major once said openly, "One kind of leader does it by example and rhetoric, others by whips. I am the latter." Hope had him canned. We laughed and enjoyed volleyball, basketball, poker, bridge, cracker-barrel philosophy, chess, books, singing, captured Japanese Suntory scotch—on and on.

I leave off on Bougainville with a most sadly remembered episode. Marines returned to their amphibious transports after extended commitment to action, exhausted by weeks of strain and tension, and weakened by weather and heavy labor. It was necessary to climb out of landing craft up the lengthy cargo nets to get thankfully and emotionally on board, out of danger. Tragically two very tired Marines could not maintain their grasp up the long ascent, and fell between the bobbing landing craft and shifting cargo net. The busy, preoccupied, landing craft crew looking up could not comprehend the desperate shouts from those high above

and looking down. It was a hell of a note on which to have to return
to Guadalcanal.

*　　*　　*

My unit got away from Bougainville and headed back to
Guadalcanal, which seemed a dreary prospect. We went right back
to our part of the Lever Brothers coconut palms plantation. It was
distant from the beach over dusty roads. And it was far from where
Eleanor Roosevelt had called, nevertheless requiring that all uri-
nals, empty artillery ammo tubes, be screened for miles up and
down the island. We conducted repeated training exercises. I func-
tioned as the survey officer and recall one tedious task—running
25 to 30 surveying legs through dense jungle, with only one talented corporal but the rest being rather elementarily educated privates. After getting through the vines, bushes, trees, and swamp
area (we called them, "Oh, shit, vines") we informed the forward
observer firing party just where we calculated the registration
point to be, where to shoot. We missed it by a mile. One of us had
wildly erred on the angle of one leg. I just concluded that this was a
useless way to go about things. Just direct those privates with their
measuring chain to locate our howitzers. Pick the target from a
photo or chart. Put me in a better job.

Indeed I got the task of organizing and training fellow lieutenants as aerial observers. Air spotters were important eyes for
field artillery, but it was not until we acquired control over some
VMO aircraft that we got to expand in this way. For some reason I
myself was not the one to get in the plane. I was told I was too tall.
Maybe, but I saw others at the task who matched my height. In the
firing batteries of a battalion the device for measuring angles, for
determining deflections, or simply pointing, was called an aiming
circle. Yet I wandered higher in this discipline, getting acquainted
with the regimental survey officer. He was from the Coast and
Geodetic Survey and operated a theodolite. Nothing important

59

eventuated here, and maybe it was just the memory of celestial navigation in Yale's NROTC unit that pushed me in this direction. I feel, however, that my experiments with the aerial observer class, aiming circles and stakes, distant aiming points, the theodolites, charts, and photo maps—somehow had a lot to do with Hope Kirk's write-ups on me in my fitness reports, propelling an offer to me of a regular commission, coming up soon.

*   *   *

After our second sojourn on Guadalcanal our battalion command group sailed for Guam in the *Rixey,* a troop transport. The firing batteries were aboard LSTs with their crews and howitzers prepared for landing in amphibian trucks, DUWKs or "ducks." Several changes were to take place on Guam for me. *Rixey* was not a ship of great comfort for the men, but lucky officers could spend their days in the officers' wardroom, the only air-conditioned space on board. It was a very boring period, the Third Marine Division convoys all steaming toward Guam till dawn and retiring to the east every day. This was for reason that the Saipan campaign was proving difficult—don't forget that necessity of keeping a reserve in readiness to help elsewhere. So we tediously sailed back and forth daily. I remember one break at Eniwetok, where practically naked troops could drink beer and play touch football with coconuts. Chinese checkers helped pass the time in the wardroom.

For the landing we had been briefed on the coral reef and beach by coast watchers. They were Australians, and their kind had previously been useful in the Solomons. Their audience was primarily we junior officers, already scheduled for the landing, so it seemed futile to tell us why we might not get across the reef. Tell it to the brass. After our rehearsals back on Guadalcanal, planned loading in appropriate landing craft, and impressive naval gunfire support, the assault went smoothly. In fact it was considered by historians to be the first, perfected amphibious landing of the war.

Not much resistance on the beach, but my headquarters of 4/12 had a surprise. A tank running laterally along the beach hit a buried aerial bomb with tip up, we then taking shelter in the lee of said tank. There were shrapnel injuries and minor, flying, coral damage to several in our reconnaissance or headquarters party. I qualified for that Purple Heart, with minor hits on my arm and face. I had the biggest black eye of all time, but truly did not need evacuation. The doc pinned the evacuation tag on me anyway, and I did not have enough sense to protest. I ended up for two days on, whatta' you know. *Rixey.*

On returning in a couple of days I had missed nothing serious. The Japs had tried to counterattack the 12th Marines, regimental command post and had done some damage, but our numbers were overwhelming in repelling the assault. There were surprises, however. One of our best corporals, a Native American Indian, was killed by a Jap hiding in the attic of a primitive hootchie. I am proud that I composed the necessary letter to his Los Angeles family. Such letters were few in field artillery, though, compared to the need in infantry. I here now and always want it known that the true heroes in combat are the members of the infantry companies. The rest of us are just fortunate, in the first place. One noon hour, in a sort of break while we snatched at our C-rations in almost the style of a picnic, suddenly a pip-squeak Jap tank came tearing through our midst. Lunch was sort of messed up, but we quickly chased and decided for him. And in another, entirely different tone and vein, it must be related that a first lieutenant Marine officer, in a night foxhole with an enlisted partner, went needlessly hysterical and in a panic shot and killed his subordinate from two feet away.

Another fortunate development for an individual and for the Marine Corps can be said to have been associated with or begun with our landing. A Guamanian lad, by name of Vincente Blaz, attached himself to a unit and stuck with it until the end of the campaign. He earned the gratitude and remained in the memory of those who could assist in his education and was to move to the continental U.S. I am careful here not to say "emigrated." Guam had always been the U.S., and there are many today sensitive to the inadequacies in our inclusion of Guamanians to full citizenship. Vincente himself became a Marine officer. I found myself alongside him later as a major in the fortress-like bunker of Third Marine Division, but now in Vietnam. He made brigadier general, served as Guam's representative in the House of Representatives, and was generously kind in recognizing me one day in my retirement.

There were important artillery moments for us on Guam, although in a matter of days the enemy had retreated to the cliffs overlooking Agana Bay. Our initial firing positions were interesting, maybe unique. Due to the generally short ranges to targets, the infantry regiment on the right got its direct support from the left artillery battalion. And, that on left, from the right, criss-crossing. While still survey officer for the 4th Battalion I did the forward reconnaissance to select our next position. On another occasion I had to convince an infantry element, confused about their location—"Here, look at the map! You are here and you'd better watch out that you don't invite some friendly fire." It was an experience to accompany a patrol getting up toward the north end of Guam, where there would be built the new, large bomber base, Harmon Field. It was to be useful in the future, for Vietnam. I watched heroic NCOs getting dog-tired Marines up on their feet after ten-minute breaks. I realized that although we were all highly motivated, most of us had luckier assignments than the simple infantry private.

In the dense undergrowth areas on Guam (small-statured) Japs, used to squatting, could scurry along through three-foot tunnels into hiding where we could not chase them. And there have to be admitted disgraceful episodes. Although many Japs committed suicide, termed "Harakiri," others could have been rounded up as prisoners, but were instead shot by Marines. Of course, orders for no more of that stuff. I watched a patrol catch one pathetic, starving Japanese prisoner, who was offered a C-ration can. He was instructed how to open it, but we were surprised that he would not handle a fork or spoon. He chose to whittle his own chopsticks from a nearby bush. A posturing Marine jokingly proffered a knife to him querying, "Harakiri?" but the watching group instinctively voiced an emphatic, compassionate, "No!"

Yes, there were changes for me. I don't recall exactly when that offer of a regular commission came in, but from then on I was USMC, no longer USMCR. Too, I had been promoted to captain. And, since there had been some casualties, there was a vacancy for a battery commander, captain's rank, in the 3rd Battalion, 12th Marines. I know my c.o., Hope Kirk, valued me, but I was to leave his outfit because he chose instead to retain the other choice, my buddy Bob Wilson, an important member of the poker game. I transferred and later when in command of my new, 3/12 battery, I was awarded in ceremony the Purple Heart, by Lt. Col. Al Bowser. He was an accomplished artillery man, wise leader, who took us to Iwo Jima and for whom I later served at Headquarters Marine Corps. Together, these changes marked my Liberation, completing my Escape From Captivity.

So, one might say that things changed from War to Peace. We had to do our part in patrolling, but the howitzers were no longer needed. With the help of Seabees, wooden decks were built for all hands. My battery area was laid out in symmetrical pattern with a clean, clear, sandy area that my first sergeant treasured as a prospective ground for battery formation. Yet it could as well make a terrific basketball court. The issue was compromised by making it a one-basket court for reversible competition. I shared my tent with another captain, close enough to the men that we could hear nighttime laughs, curses, vulgarities, and once this wailing. "Yeah, look at us in this goddamn, piss-ant hell hole of Guam. Think of all them bastards in Europe, with all those dames, booze, good times."

We generally stuck to our bivouac area, yet there was exploring to do. We became familiar with other parts of Guam, the other beachhead where a Marine brigade and an Army division had landed. We utilized Guam's severely damaged Agana Hospital for minor medical needs. There was a spot commemorating where the navigator, Ferdinand Magellan had landed, and we knew about but suppressed our curiosity about the secret, new, submarine base or cove which Marines now could offer to the navy. The navy set about enlarging and improving Apra Harbor, although it was confined and, I never believed, became much of a major port. In time Admiral Nimitz moved his headquarters to the cliffs above Agana (also, let us say, courtesy of the Third Marine Division). Guam was the first U.S. bit of territory to be liberated from the Japanese in WW II.

We got settled in garrison in the center of the island, which was sort of peanut-shaped. There was a missionary chapel nearby, and we inherited a shack to serve as the officers' mess and club. We enjoyed tents with wooden decks built by our Seabee pals (A payoff to them was a part of a large cache of Japanese Suntory whiskey.) Field artillery could corner this treasure with their trucks. When ordered by the division to turn it all in by next day, sure enough, that morning all the bottles had disappeared. We had movies every night on the same grounds for baseball by day. Training for the next event continued, and Guam offered vast empty countryside for infantry maneuver but not artillery fire. I watched one day an infantry regiment being rehearsed on a training mission to "reach that high ground and hold it." It was a hot, tedious, and difficult day. Near its end the tough commander, especially critical of some squads that had not been taking cover as they should, ordered that the maneuver be done all over again. Yes, tough, but he was intent on training to save their lives another day.

Guam was north of the equator so we felt that we were better participating in that advance upon Japan, island-skipping now rather than the step-by-step process. No Jap air bothered us. We got our share of torrential rains, but the scene was healthy. However, there was dengue fever. This was called "breakbone," a high intensive fever but lasting only a short time. On New Year's Eve of 1944–1945 I had another flare-up of malaria and had to miss one of our good evenings. There was that ration of beer for all hands, maybe more than that in the officers' mess. Anyone who did not consume his allotment found that he could not save it over until another day. (Plenty of others to see that that did not occur.) We had some pretty good performers. A favorite ballad started, "Oh, what a glorious thought I am thinking, concerning that Great Speckled Bird. . . . "

*   *   *

Getting underway for Iwo there were a couple of minor incidents before embarkation. There was a joint club or recreation area where there congregated hundreds of Marines and many numbers of Gen. Curtis LeMay's gallant 15th Air Force personnel. The B-29s were already bombing and fire-blasting the cities in Japan, and we were destined for a pretty big showdown with the Nips. I'll just say it was the biggest beer bust of all time. There were thereafter the first Iwo Jima casualties, guys having jeep accidents on the way home. At embarkation our commanding general, the Big E, Maj. Gen. Graves B. Erskine (the Gen. George Patton of the Marine Corps), ordered all to hike to the ships, a last insistence upon our readiness, training, hardening, conditioning. Some units did not get the word and got caught by M.P.s when the troops used trucks. Somehow we artillerymen got away with rides to the port.

Moving north from Guam on a navy transport my artillery battalion was loaded on top of the 3rd Marines, the infantry regiment intended for us to support. We had trained with them, and our forward observers were ready to live with and assist them. However, that organization which had long been overseas, including Fiji, was designated for reserve. There was no such thing as a reserve of artillery. Use it or lose it, so we were loaded on top, ready to be last in, first out. Ultimately that regiment was not committed to action, and we went ashore without them. So might one ask, did not this make the Iwo operation that much more difficult and costly to the rest of the three divisions engaged? Maybe, and Marines could be sympathetic for other Marines held out of the action. But who knows how their preserved readiness might affect the timetable and aggressive strategy for the next operation—Okinawa? And the sooner Okinawa, the sooner the War would itself be over, and other lives saved.

En route there was no secrecy about our destination. In fact we could conjecture all about our futures in little copies of *Time* magazine. Veterans who had made the earlier operations were relaxed enough, but I experienced one relationship that stood out. I had a pre-landing association, which was to be climaxed fifty years later. Our battalion doctor had just joined us. He had had no earlier combat experience. He was a devout Jesuit, older than I, and we often spoke of spiritual matters, bravery, and courage. I assumed he would have great strength when we hit the sands.

Skip to a distant place and a later time, when I peered at a menu board in a busy hospital in Los Angeles catching a familiar name. Could it be the same doctor? A go-between M.D. assured me that my guy had retired, no longer practiced at this address, but offered to find him for me. Within hours the phone rang, and indeed it was my doctor. His immediate and emphatic first words were to recount how he, the well-educated Jesuit, a naval officer, had been fearful and very uncertain about being able to function at our Iwo landing. He had been impressed and restored to effectiveness, just by being around Marines, presumably including me. He, with the assumed strong spiritual strength, was very insistent and repetitious in this. Difference was that Marines had to take care of subordinates—and unlike the doc we had been through this stuff before.

Historians of the Iwo Jima campaign report that we were deprived of the full tonnage of naval gunfire support that had been planned, but the retort was that this would not have made a great difference and that the naval elements had to depart early for other operations. We climbed on shore over very steep beaches and up terraced levels of black sand. There was great damage from water and wind to landing craft. Coxswains could not hold their positions straight on the steep beaches in the crashing surf. It became so rough that for a couple of days landing craft could only beach on the opposite shore. Jap counter fire did not start right away, but soon beaches were a congested mess of landed equipment. The reloading of the wounded for evacuation in those landing craft was the priority for harassed shore party personnel. We took positions below the edge of the runway of the old Jap airfield, and pretty soon crippled B-29s trying to get back from Japan to Guam, crash-landed right next to us. Too, hospital evacuation planes would land very close. We glimpsed nurses, first females we had seen for over two years! A memory is of the tanks laboring in the loose sands of Iwo. They had phones and trapdoors on their bottoms—it was a godsend that they occasionally could pick up a casualty who was otherwise unreachable. Flamethrowers were most valuable of weapons. A big scare occurred when a major ammunition dump was set ablaze one night. There was a false rumor that the war in Europe was over. A lot of weapons were needlessly fired that night.

It was once said that the safest place in the world was behind a Marine battalion, but wait a minute. That is in a defensive situation. Here the most dangerous of zones were those areas between rear units and the front lines themselves. Evacuations for the wounded were tough, for each infantry battalion only had two jeeps for all their needs. A big protest in my book is that another artillery battalion than mine was committed to battle with mere 75-mm pack howitzers, in this most ferocious of actions. That is to say, pop guns, designed in 1898, to be broken down into loads and transported into battle by mules. Meanwhile, in the European theatre others were getting the best and the biggest of new and large caliber howitzers and guns.

There were no 3rd Marines ashore with whom I would have had to effect liaison, but we sent forward observers up to assist other infantry. Aerial observation craft got aloft, and we could listen to their transmissions but there were few identifiable targets for them. I had it easy. We were ordered to land light, but our battery mess sergeant fashioned in a miniature cook stove, smuggled fresh food, and provided a couple of cots—none of that C or K ration stuff. Again don't get me wrong—Marine officers, we proudly say, were trained to put their men's welfare before their own. Remember, "Never ask a man to do something that you are not willing to do yourself." But the mess sergeant could not break out his own cot unless he had also taken care of me. My shelter halves were oriented to form a perfect triangular framing of Mount Suribachi. There was cheering when the flag went up. We'd been issued field jackets for the cold weather to be expected, but my unit was surprised to find the sands were hot in our area. You know, up to your butts in hot lava sand and freezing to death above the waist. Eventually there were hitched up limited water showers in this hot sands area. But there appeared a big difference in the island's perfect teardrop configuration when we returned for a reunion in 1995. We were very surprised on that return to find that there was now a prolongation of the hot sands projecting into the ocean, spoiling the symmetry.

Meeting other acquaintances that one might know from earlier times among the thousands of us ashore was rare, but I recount a pair of such encounters. On Guam I had a cook, a messman, who was impatient and disconsolate in his assigned job, and wanted a transfer. He informed me that he was a saxophone player and aspired to join the Third Division band. So off he had gone, only later to be spotted by me on the black sands of Iwo. What happened to bandsmen in combat? He had been drafted into stretcher-bearing duty. He remarked to me that certainly he had been glad to get out of the galley but that he did not know that a saxophone player would end up as he.

Too, I accidentally ran into an old pal, dating back to when we were teenagers together at Hotchkiss school. His father had been a minister and I felt then, as indeed it turned out later, that Bill would end up in divinity school and eventually in the pulpit. That day on Iwo he was virtually unrecognizable. He told me that in truth, literally, his hair had just turned snow white overnight. At the finish the Big E ordered a pretty spectacular move. There had not previously been a major, night assault in the Pacific war. The Big E surprised and finished off the conquest of Iwo by such an order, a final tough assignment for the 9th and 21st Marines, in the center of the Corps front.

My most emotional moment, at a 1995 reunion? I was with a veteran, a pal, who had intimately participated in the infantry assault on Suribachi and had gone on to earn high rank, Maj. Gen. Fred Haynes. His company was the one which first surmounted Suribachi and planted the flag. We noted a lonely and sorrowful lady near us, who seemed upset that no one was paying attention to her. We Marines were remembering a Jap heavy weapon in a cave that had hindered or held up the Suribachi assault. A navy destroyer had ventured in close to give Marines support. The Jap weapon surprised all by getting off a round that hit the DD bridge, only causing minimum casualties. One casualty, however, was the captain himself. The lady was his daughter. The mood was very emotional—remembering the naval captain who had gone into harm's way to help us.

When it was our turn to depart Iwo, we were assigned to a merchant marine vessel, manned by others than our naval service. We all realized that the emergency lift only allowed ordinary treatment, bunks, and chow, but this last lift was certainly an anti-climax. We were glad to get home again—that is, to Guam.

SIX

Learning Chinese at Berkeley and Using It in Peking and Tsingtao

On Iwo one day we got welcome mail call. I heard from my old college roommate, Jack Duncan (then a lieutenant in the army), that he was headed for the University of California at Berkeley to attend an instruction course in Chinese. He reported that it sounded like a great idea and that all services were participating. After the war he was to go to the China-Burma-India Theatre and ended up backloading ships to return surplus supplies and materiel from Calcutta to the U.S. I reasoned that after Iwo and a little time back in the U.S. I would have to battle the Nips in China. So, my course was different.

We returned to Guam from Iwo, my group still pretty intact. It was depressing, however, to visit certain infantry battalions to look up friends, only to find that the turnover of personnel was almost one hundred percent, casualties or rotation home. We artillerymen relieved some other Marines, taking our turn in trying to chase stray Japs still hiding out in the Guam bush. And one day the radio announced that President Roosevelt had died. It was an emotional announcement for us overseas combat vets, and I was shocked to return home to hear some dismiss the president with, "He was a traitor to his class." I flew home via Hawaii at about the same time as his son, James, and headed first for Headquarters Marine Corps, Washington, where I got to see the commandant. This was Gen. Thomas Holcomb, who had himself been a lan-

70

guage student in the Peking, post-Boxer Rebellion period, but maybe still in the time of the Empress Dowager. My application for language school was approved and that got me a little extra leave returning to California. V-E Day was a big event, but for me arriving at Berkeley the significant events were the atomic bomb drops, the surrender, and most soldiers and sailors heading home to be civilians. We who stayed in the service earned the title of "lifers."

I was surprised to find myself committed to a year-and-a-half course and considered myself lucky that the Hiroshima and Nagasaki atomic bomb drops meant the end of the war. I could stay in uniform for the intellectual challenge and the physical adventure of China. But when I applied, I did not know that the course might put me in a painful position. Was I to be a schoolboy while my comrades were sent on to more, the invasion of Japan? The army soon phased most of its students out of Berkeley. I generally categorize my fellow students into three groups. There were some young Chinese-American students desirous of studying their heritage and language, perhaps to venture on to China in business or trade. They were shy, retiring, seemingly uncommitted to serious study. There were as well several Jesuit priests who were destined for missionary futures in China. Fine, they said, but we have the rest of our lives to learn this language. They seemed a bit lazy, but they were pleasant, educated company. And then there was our group of about a dozen Marines, some volunteers, some popped into the course because of family background, or some simply because they had regular commissions. I pay tribute now to some of those remembered classmates—Swede Larsen, Ralph Powell, Barney McLean, Tom Dutton, Bill James, Jack Lindsay, and John Bristow. Our group was naturally competitive. We threw ourselves into the work, relished mah-jongg, and did not care if we made up puns or committed mistakes.

Learning Chinese, oral and written, was formidable. One had to grasp that many individual words sounded the same and had to be given a certain tone or lilt. They had to be used in combinations to make sense. If you have never thought about it, try to figure out how to set Chinese into newsprint or for a typewriter, or how to use a dictionary, or index a book. The course had been set up at the university by Dr. Winston Pettus, a veteran missionary, as a home for the College of Chinese Studies. This was a Peking school driven out of its home on Morrison Street and given a new wartime life in Berkeley. There was for us a touch of following in the trace of Marine Corps, post-Boxer Rebellion, or legation guard duty in Peking. Chinese is traditionally a task of rote memorization, often just, "Go ahead, student, and learn this. Later you will understand what it means." There are wonderful examples solidly in my consciousness that have stayed with me over the years. One goes something like: "Live a long life, study all your life, but there will be an enormity that you have not learned." Another favorite, "One man alone is cold, but in the group, together, there is warmth."

*　　*　　*

It was January 1947, as in San Francisco I awaited transportation to China. It was announced that Gen. George Marshall was giving up the task of trying to get the Chinese Communists and Nationalists to kiss and make up. (He was to become President Truman's secretary of state.) I worried a bit that this meant America was giving up and I would not get to China. Not so. With a couple of other companions I was embarked on the *Repose,* a hospital ship. The *Repose* was not to be employed as a troopship, per the Geneva Convention, so we Marines were billeted as patients in the psycho ward, where we entertained ourselves with Chinese checkers and mah-jongg.

Arrived at Peking, I was assigned to the 2nd Battalion, 5th Marines, First Marine Division. Our forces were being shrunken down—after all, what was the mission?—and artillery was no longer needed. We had one company sort of patrolling the railroad lines of North China, one company guarding the airfield, and a third just covering home plate on military police duty. It seemed that about half the outfit would go on liberty one night, while the rest did a little MP duty supervising them. Next night, roles might be swapped. There were accidents to be investigated, dirty restaurants to be declared off-limits, whorehouses to be shut down, and stolen goods, principally jeeps, to be recovered.

In my duty as an assistant provost marshal, I was kept busy in this stolen vehicle business. The Chinese would grab a jeep in Peking and scuttle it down to Tientsin. Meanwhile the Tientsin thieves would send their finds up to Peking. We had elaborate lists of body and engine numbers to prove precise ownership, and of course it was blatantly obvious from markings that these vehicles were USMC property. The Chinese might seize on one digit as erroneous, blurred, or missing in a lengthy listing so that they could contend that no, this was not a jeep that had to be returned. On one occasion to overcome this stalling, I hit upon the trick of swiping the jeep engine rotor to prevent its being driven away.

At the higher levels, above or outside of that of the 2nd Battalion, Fifth Marines, there were other commands with differing objectives or purposes. They were centered in the majestic, archaic Peking Hotel. The first floor housed Chiang K'ai-shek's Nationalists; second floor, the Communists of Mao Tse-tung and Chou En-lai; and the third, the group of U.S. officers trying to adjudicate China's gathering civil war. Disrespectfully we referred to that third floor group as "The Hall of a Hundred Sleeping Colonels." The facts were that the war was over, many high-ranking officers had nothing else to do, and the Japs had been repatriated. America's effort to bring Nats and Reds together was failing, and we had no true mission nor purpose.

*　　*　　*

However, there were many opportunities for learning, for

amusement, and for gaining of experience in these years in China. I found myself with an older subordinate, Bill Schwerin, a true and proven warrior on Guadalcanal and Tarawa, but busted from major to master sergeant. He added the aristocratic "Von" to his last name, so perhaps this helped him meet and attract a German lady, girlfriend, Hanna Woidt. And she was a scholar and an artist and an author on China. Measures of her superiority were facts that her parents had sent her to England for upbringing away from the Teutons in WW I, that she gave warmth and friendship to several European Jews in Peking, and that she had long been separated from her Nazi husband. He had been hauled off for war crimes and helping the Japanese. I enjoyed so much the company and hospitality of Von and Hanna, when I visited them in her authentic, charming home. A particular meeting was with Charolotte Horstmann, a Jewish refugee from Hitler. She eventually was to get out of China, to Hong Kong, where she established a magnificent art and antique gallery. One evening after Mozart on an ancient Victrola, I mentioned to a couple of supposed German innocents that I was an assistant provost marshal. Next morning they decamped six hundred miles to the west, fearing that I must certainly be on their tails as other war criminals.

Hanna's home was one-story, the dirt floor covered with magnificent Peking rugs, on an alley where the peddlers and entertainers colorfully announced their wares with various street cries, whistles, gongs, or drums. Spin forward with me, maybe forty years, to when I found myself in a taxicab in what you are now meant to call Beijing, rolling up a very broad boulevard. There were new, high-rise buildings and hotels on my right and the old, crowded, so distinctly different, one-story structures like Hanna's and the colorful alleys on my left. I realized that I was traveling on the trace of Peking's massive, eastern city wall. Historic, unequalled, symmetrical Peking had had to give way to the explosion of population growth. It took a while to realize what had once occupied that boulevard space. The loss of that wall for me seemed almost personal. Peking had a grid pattern from its founding by Kubalai Khan, arranged in marvelous symmetry. Inner lakes and streams all flowed south through the fabled Sewer Gate through which the Brits had entered to relieve the besieged compounds during Boxer time. In 1947 this Marine Corps captain being pulled along by a laboring, sweating, cheerful ricksha coolie was delighted to direct him, not, "At the next corner turn right" or maybe, "Take the second left." All understood simply, "Go north" or, "To the west."

The German lady, far from being a Nazi, took us once to her nearby weekend vacation spot in the Western Hills outside of the city. Although there was hardly any danger from the Ba-Lus, stemming from "Eighth Route Army," as the communist military were termed, I was advised to tell servants and others that I was a Frenchman. In the area was the renowned Chala Mission, where monks who reminded me of Disney's Seven Dwarfs ran a superb winery. They could produce every variety of splendid wines, but sorry, there was no champagne. Cork from Portugal was not available. Hanna at our picnic lunch told the coolie to put the bottles in the well for cooling. He did exactly that, only complication being that they went to the very bottom with no means of recovery. What a perfect, obedient servant.

Returning to Peking before the massive, impressive, guardian gates should be closed for the night, Hanna, Von, and I had an unmatched encounter with an aged peasant. Just to be familiar, for certainly we knew the answer, we asked him, "Which way, Old Brother, is the way to Peking?" As is the Chinese way, there could not be an initial, specific answer to our clear question. He had to ask about our homes, how many children we had, what were our occupations, what the weather might be. This went on back and forth repeatedly. Finally we asked again the question. His reply to us foreigners (with our peculiar faces and big noses, intruders into his Chinese universe). "You cannot have the answer to that question." Next, our "Why not, Old Brother?" He, "Because you don't speak Chinese." And our natural, "Well, in what language is it that we are conversing, Old Brother?" only produced a slack-jawed, open-mouth gaping. He, perhaps never having met or conversed with a "Big Nose" foreigner, simply lived on another planet than we.

*   *   *

Then there came a time when the Marines were to be withdrawn from Peking. George Carrington with his budding competency and interest in Chinese and China was not looking forward to the thought of being uselessly assigned to Guam. So I took it upon myself to jigger up a little artificial, medical complaint which could allow me to venture down to Tsingtao. There was stationed the familiar hospital ship *Repose,* but my real purpose was to visit the Marine Corps command. Fleet Marine Corps, Western Pacific. It was just a small, symbolic organization, with reduced units and no field artillery, but it was commanded by Col. Sam Griffith, old China hand and more, a veteran Chinese linguist. I was hopeful that he would be sympathetic to my plea for a transfer which would allow me to enjoy Tsingtao, vice Guam. When I got back to Peking, lo and behold—I don't know whether it was Sam's doings or an independent request—the U.S. Navy, on board the command ship, *Eldorado,* needed an assistant intelligence officer. I would have preferred the shore with Marines, but things were to work out O.K. I did not have to go to Guam.

So I found myself in Tsingtao in the service of the U.S. Navy. As an assistant intelligence officer I worked for Capt. Eddie Pearce, a Japanese language officer outside of the area in which he might have preferred to be. It was peacetime for us Yanks but a time of turmoil for China as Mao steadily ran Chiang's forces out of town. Perhaps it was not real war, although millions perished in China's revolution. However, there were some peculiar events that I include in this account.

76

Col. Sam Griffith had been an investigator, perhaps a translator of Sun Tze, author of *The Art of War*. In it we learn that the wise general who has surrounded his enemy always should leave one side of the square open so that his opponent might escape. Fight to the death? What a silly notion. In a confirming observation of this we could sometimes suspect that "silver bullets" were utilized. A wily commander could see that his troops might be switched to the other side. Another traditional practice of Chinese armies was to ensure that Manchurians, for example, served in South China. And, that southerners would be assigned to an area of this vast land where they could not speak the local dialect. They could never defect nor run away. They were totally dependent upon their commander, the warlord.

The token force of U.S. military could not do much about the war, yet there was an incident of participation for me. A Marine Corps aviation formation of six, old, propeller-driven planes one day got caught in a thunderstorm off and over a spot called Goose Bay, up the Shantung coast a bit from Tsingtao. Most got back safely, but one pilot crash-landed. He truly was rescued and given sympathetic help, by the peasants. However, our nervous reaction was to furiously dive-bomb the villagers, albeit with flour sacks. This assistant intelligence officer, with his rudimentary knowledge of Chinese but with some understanding of how the other side might think, was sent with Alfredo Canaverro, a Macao, Portuguese-Chinese, consummate linguist and negotiator, to get our pilot back. The naval landing force, from the cruiser *Saint Paul,* made up primarily of very young sailors, not fully trained, frightened that World War III was starting, fired off their weapons in wild confusion. In this anti-Communist era even innocent, helpful peasants in the countryside were to be regarded as devils incarnate.

We palavered for several days. The innocent villagers were followed by a local militia force, but eventually true Reds arrived. It was a most tedious, boring time, we having daily to make long trips ashore by landing craft across shallow Goose Bay. The Communists alleged, after the flour-sack bombing runs and the landing force invasion, prelude to war itself—"Scores of women have suffered miscarriages, hundreds of children have been orphaned, and thousands have fled from their homes. A million dollars is demanded in payment for the peasants' distress." This meant ransom, something not to be considered in the spirit of that time. George Carrington eventually bargained for return of the pilot in exchange for a handout of medical and food supplies. This took several echelons of U.S. Navy and State Department commands off the hook—from Tsingtao, Nanking, Pearl Harbor, back to Washington. I said I regretted the incident. The pilot, Lt. Dick Winters, a personal pal, strode back one evening for a marvelous, celebratory Chinese banquet that included our contribution of Johnny Walker Black Label. The red-hots and we Yanks declared ourselves comrades for life. There was fallout, however. On my fitness report was inscribed, "Carrington did an exceptional job, marred only by an authorized apology to the Communists." (That's the kiss of death if and when one comes up for highest promotion.) However, do not get me wrong. Marines know that, "There but for the grace of God go I." There are many other stumbling blocks along the way—death, accident, disease, lousy commanding officers, prejudice, favoritism, bad assignments, just bad luck . . .

*   *   *

In this recitation of my life in Tsingtao. I would be remiss if I failed to include the fact that I was married there. Antonia was a good lady, a U.S. Army secretary to Army Maj. Gen. Lawrence Keiser, stationed in Nanking. The ceremony was in Tsingtao, in a traditional Lutheran church with a Navy chaplain and our friends in attendance. We tried for twenty years. I was a straight arrow.

But after Vietnam we divorced. I trust it is O.K. to get on with my naval exposure or experience in Tsingtao.

*   *   *

There was a change of commanders of Naval Forces, Western Pacific, that brought us Vice Adm. Oscar Badger. He had the aristocratic aura of the wearer of the purple, for having won the Congressional Medal of Honor at Veracruz in 1911. Having been born in the Naval Gun Factory, in D.C., he liked to say he was a "son of a gun." His current aide was a bit of a cry-baby and wanted to go home. So, all of a sudden I was assigned as the new aide-de-camp, or flag lieutenant. I had an exciting ride with this new boss. I accompanied him to Peking, where he tried valiantly to assist the Chinese Nationalists. A remembered general was known as the "Christian General," who baptized his troops with a fire hose. I went along on trips to Shanghai and Nanking, sitting in on meetings with our sweet, frail, ex-missionary, Ambassador Leighton Stuart. Also, with Chiang K'ai-shek himself, whose Chinese accent, it was said, many subordinates could not comprehend. To my ear it was simply, "Hao, Hao, Hao, Hao," on and on, meaning "good." And I was along at a very personal moment when Admiral Badger called on his counterpart in Japan, Gen. Douglas MacArthur. The admiral for China advised the general for Japan that he might soon have to order all dependents out of China.

Anticipating what was to come, Admiral Badger took the flagship and other naval vessels on an extensive reconnaissance cruise, to investigate where Chiang might displace his regime. En route I got a teasing from fellow officers who challenged me on my ability as flag lieutenant to hoist signal flag orders to the so-called task force. We called in the Chushan Islands, not far off Shanghai and Chekiang province, islands that would have been an unlikely destination for Chiang. Singapore, Manila, and Brunei

79

were interesting. However, our true investigation was what we then called Formosa, but now call Taiwan. It was destined to be important for me.

In 1948 the Formosan scene still had a flavor of Japan's fifty years of occupation, but thousands of Chinese mainlanders had begun to arrive. In later historical study I came to appreciate that Taiwan had always been an overflow outlet for wars, disease, floods, famine, overpopulation, or rebellions on the mainland. Some would term this new wave as carpetbaggers, but in fact they were just military and civilians fleeing from Mao Tse-tung, for good reason. There had been a nasty, violent, repressive massacre of a reported 10,000 native Taiwanese on 2/22, notoriously remembered as happening on the 22nd day of the second month of 1948. It had become generally known, but perhaps not in its full seriousness and magnitude. At the flagship gangway I was one day surprised by an apparent intellectual, maybe a journalist, who thrust his reporting upon me, hoping I would send it to *The New York Times*. I guess I pushed it merely into the naval intelligence system.

*   *   *

Finally, in spring of 1949 it came time for all Yanks to get out of Tsingtao. Our presence was felt for a bit longer in Shanghai and Nanking. Chiang's government moved to Chungking. I tell of my saddling up, or weighing anchor, in a personal manner. It was a desperate time for the starving refugees in Tsingtao. Some were eating the bark off the trees. As we Marines got ready to bail out, what was I to do about my beloved dog, a true Tibetan Lhasa Apso? But I solved my problem. I gave her to the big, bad, communist, Russian, consul general, who was really a pretty good guy with the good Russian name of Lelchitsky, along with a thousand tins of sardines at a penny a tin, as we closed down the post exchange.

The Far East

Teachers, Jesuits, And A few Marines, U.C. Berkeley

The Peking Wall And Sewer Gate

Provost Marshal, Peking

Officers Of 3rd Bn, 11th Marines, Korea

High-angle Fire, Korea

Chinese Marine Corps, Taiwan

Taipei, Taiwan

Awarded A Chinese Medal

SEVEN

HQMC, G-2; and a Trip
to the Persian Gulf

In the spring of 1949 I had returned home from China, after Admiral Badger released me from my assignment as aide. In fact, he gave me a special hop on his aircraft from Tsingtao to Okinawa. This was an interesting stop for me, Iwo Jima having been the closeout for my participation in WW II. At Naha, Okinawa, I got to see my first jet aircraft, these just coming into service at the time. My orders were to Headquarters Marine Corps. I do not remember why I was chosen for this, but it seemed a good next duty station for a captain. The Marine Corps had shrunk down in numbers in this post-war time, and either the headquarters did not know what else to do with me or it was my China time that propelled me into the G-2 section.

I recount my first tour at HQMC in this chapter. My assignment was in intelligence. Mao was driving Chiang from the mainland onto Taiwan. The Korean War was soon to break out. Our nation's interest and preoccupation was upon China, Korea, and Japan.

* * *

HQMC was in the Navy Annex, Arlington, and it felt just a bit different from the Pentagon and D.C. itself, across the Potomac River. My geographic locale being always of interest to me, I explain where I found myself. We were close to Arlington Cemetery and the home of Robert E. Lee. The Columbia Pike led west via Bailey's Crossroads to the converted barn, home, I found on Braddock Road in Fairfax Courthouse. Along the turnpike there still existed an unincorporated, forlorn cluster of shacks or cabins, serving as homes for black descendants of slaves. During one severe winter, within yards of help from the well-traveled turnpike, one person had frozen to death. Certainly the memorials, paths, and the aura of the Arlington Cemetery evoked memory of important figures in our nation's history. We know of Lee. General Braddock was George Washington's early worry during the revolution. John Singleton Mosby with his raiders surprised a Yankee general in his bed one night—in the house now become the Episcopal rector's Fairfax residence.

Getting to my military life and duties later, let me hint of my home-from-China pleasures and routine. Fairfax had an old-fashioned feel to it. There was a feed store for animals. Routine at the local bank, which held my mortgage, was so simple that the management refused to send out statements because of the expense of stamps. I was invited to the Fairfax Hunt Ball, although there was nothing horsey about it. Venturing a bit abroad one could charter a boat in the Chesapeake and visit Annapolis. On Sundays I played on a suburban Washington, soccer team that got me out of town. The eastern shore of Maryland seemed another world before a bay bridge brought it back in touch. One two-story home, set well apart from the road in a meadow had been a Civil War headquarters, Union or Confederate? In the attic one could see the initials, scribblings, and diagrams left by billeted soldiers. We had excursions to rural Virginia, charming spots such as Charlottesville, Culpepper, and Gordonsville.

A rediscovered acquaintance from China was an interesting friend. He was Victor Kamkin, an anti-Soviet Russian who had led the community of White Russians in Tsingtao and had published our *North China Marine* periodical. We had helped him find refuge in the U.S., but he now was enduring tough times trying to run a boarding house near Bailey's Crossroads. Victor theorized that the Chinese had no sense of censorship nor guarding against transmission of the written word. He thought that it would be easy to communicate with contacts in Manchuria and North China. In time we got him a Russian typewriter, introduced him to the CIA, and shifted him out of the boarding house business. He was to open a Russian bookstore near their embassy in D.C., in hopeful belief that embassy employees might occasionally drift in for chatting, if not true disclosure of anything important.

*   *   *

My duties in the G-2 Section revolved about reading the many reports from all types of military and naval commands, attaches, and other agencies all over the world. Those adjudged important were extracted or filed. This often required specific classification. Restricted, Confidential, or Secret. Distinguishing between these became so tedious and inconsequential that it often became easiest just to call everything Secret, or help me, Top Secret. When told to write up my own job description, I impertinently included the task of reading the daily newspapers. I had companions in this sub-section, an aged veteran from the State Department, a fellow Marine who wore the wings of an aviator, and a jolly, young civilian from the civil service system. We were responsible for a weekly briefing on world trouble spots before the commandant and staff. When the Korean War broke out, with Marines quickly committed, we had interesting topics or details to convey. We wrote staff studies. We attended debriefings—that is to say, interrogations, story telling, or lectures by returned attaches or CIA personnel. I recall laboring over a study of the beaches of friendly Denmark, in detail—many words and interpretation of aerial photographs. Were we thinking of amphibious landings at the start of WW III or were we just being kept busy because these

Danish maps and charts had fallen into our possession? It is a small country, the first in the world, it was said, to be completely mapped, probably by the German occupiers of WW II.

*   *   *

For an interval there was a relief from the tedium of peacetime headquarters duty by assignment to a U.S. Army course over the river in Main Navy. The course was termed Strategic Intelligence School. I surmise today that the several service commands just filled quotas, rather than having true needs for this. I am disrespectful, I concede, but there are two specific items remembered today, taught then at SIS. A very impassioned and emphatic major general from the new U.S. Air Force lectured this assembly of junior officers that best national strategic policy was to wage an immediate, preemptive, nuclear strike against the Soviet Union. Rather shocking. I wonder who reined him in. Another lecture was sort of a briefing on the vulnerabilities of the United States in a WW III. We had it pointed out to us that sabotage or a taking out of the nearby, railroad bridge of the Richmond, Fredericksburg, and Potomac RR would be of overwhelming importance in case of the outbreak of a new war. This would constitute a horrendous logistical problem, necessitating rerouting of all rail transportation far to the west. Somehow we students could not be very alarmed at the thought.

*   *   *

In early 1950, a remarkable tour or reconnaissance was organized by HQMC. Representatives from the several staff sections were selected to go on what you might call an expedition to the Middle East. There was a heavier balance of aviators over ground officers, in the numbers of a general and a few colonels. The mission was to investigate the vulnerabilities of the important oil fields, and our potential to sabotage or to deny them to the Soviets,

90

in case they made good on their historic threat to break out through the Black Sea or Iran. We flew in a R5D, a big-capacity, four-propeller, naval-configured aircraft, making calls in London and for some reason, Malta. We made Tobruk in Libya, Cyprus, and Habbaniya, a British-occupied airfield near Basra. A veteran missionary intercepted me with an invitation to accompany him to see the Gardens of Babylon. Intriguing, but an impossible diversion for this young captain. A valuable lesson learned, however, was from a senior Brit. When I frugally answered that I'd like a beer, he supervised me, "Young man, in this part of the world you drink a pink gin."

The significant destination was Bahrain, where the U.S. Navy command was on board a small but importantly air-conditioned vessel designed as a tender for seaplanes. We ventured further into Saudi Arabia itself, discovering Dhahran as just a small center, overwhelmingly dominated by oil—nearby wells, pipelines, and loading terminals for tankers. There were no roads. Oil was just poured out on the desert sand, stabilizing a roadbed only marginally. I can only describe our purpose and mission as silly. Recalling that it was envisioned as obstructing a Russian drive for the airfields and oil wells, we got out our pencils and notebooks. What could we ask or investigate? "Are the natives friendly?" "How long is the runway?" "What is the weather like?"

Also in Bahrain I experienced a strongly remembered episode of law in the Muslim world. We were on liberty playing softball. Someone had left a warm-up jacket on a bench, a very petty one, and a thief, picked it up and was caught. He was hauled off, the authorities declaring that the punishment would hardly be petty. His right hand, his feeding hand, would be cut off. I cannot say that this was actually carried out. However, this was the drastic threat, the report, that we heard about these people, these times, and this practice of the Muslim world.

I leave this Persian Gulf adventure with items that may instruct or entertain, but are probably not consequential. During

WW II the defense of oil was based on maintenance of a destroyer in the Gulf for the benefit of King Ibn Saud. A Colonel Eddy, a rare Arabic specialist and USMC of course, nurse-maided it into as luxurious a floating suite as possible, an important inclusion being a herd of sheep to ensure a plentiful supply of mutton at all times.

In Arabia water was adjudged a gift of Allah, its free flow in the desert and even by underwater outlets in the Persian Gulf never to be impeded. When outsiders would cap wells in this parched land, oil or water, nomad Arabs would honor the oil, but knock the water caps asunder. Also, in the desert, temperatures tended to rise so high that an inadequately secured pipeline might writhe and move like a snake. The solution was not to fiddle with ordinary supports but to lock the line permanently into the most solid of firm, strong, permanent pedestals.

In this Persian Gulf we had a local representative or host, a USMC lieutenant colonel. One of his jobs was to test the bearing of the salt-encrusted, shoreline soil. In case of future military action, say running a convoy up to Kuwait, could trucks or tanks be operated without breaking down through the crust? For this question he utilized a penetrometer, a device to measure depth and firmness of the soil beneath. He was an accomplished golfer and possessed a Saluki, akin to the Afghan hound. In that forlorn desert landscape he could help pass the boring days with long, smashed drives, the Saluki bounding ahead to recover his golf balls.

Yes, this trip was interesting, and we participants from different jobs and desks at HQMC got to know each other in relaxed and companionable style. I concede that I have treated this Middle Eastern venture of Yanks lightly. It was peacetime. Those Soviets were frightful, but they were not threatening us meaningfully. "Boondoggle" signifies a trivial, useless, or wasteful project or activity. It turned out, or we always knew it at the time, that the true purpose of our expedition was to justify the retention of the R5D, for use by the Commandant of the Marine Corps for Air. Use it or lose it.

*   *   *

Back in Washington, back to our staff jobs at HQMC, and a bit later the Korean War was in full swing. I was designated to get over to the Pentagon early each morning to a teletype conference with General MacArthur's command in Japan. There were some heroic and some tragic battles to report. I still held my low rank, but in the darkness of some of those early morning teletype sessions with Tokyo and Korea, I would see beside me the four stars of Gen. Matthew Ridgeway. After early setbacks his leadership was to save the day. I would take the Marine Corps teletype copy back to headquarters, where all were concerned with the welfare of fellow Marines. Once, the FBI paid a call. It seemed that some had leaked reports—of an invidious, denigrating, contrasting nature—to Drew Pearson, and I could only assure that it was not I.

When my tour in G-2 was tapering off, I fully expected that it would be my turn for Korean combat. However, I was surprised by an assignment to the Naval Intelligence School in nearby Anacostia, Maryland. Sure, I was still committed to China, but we eager, motivated warriors all aspired for orders to Korea. The forces were being built up, reserves called to active duty, so I did not appreciate this diversion to be a schoolboy again. At Anacostia I had a reunion with fellow officers, USMC and USN, who, like me, had been through language training before. At first, trying to pick up Chinese again, there were some awkward blanks, dead ends. For some reason (and this really seemed peculiar), my school and college French would come out. We progressed, however, though I felt I had had enough provost marshal, aide to an admiral, G-2 stuff and wanted to get back to my field artillery business. The instruction was important, but we knew that real proficiency emerged only when one was truly in the field, trying to say "it" in Chinese, with Chinese. One of our instructors had an accent that had little relationship to Mandarin, so we did not make great progress with him. Maybe we made it up by enthusiastic mah-jongg over the noon hours. One guy would get the tiles; another, set up the tables and chairs; next, the sandwiches; and the fourth, the Cokes.

EIGHT

Korea, War and Truce

I had been in WW II. I had been in China. I had had a tour of duty in the G-2 Section of Headquarters Marine Corps. Now it was time for me to get back into the Fleet Marine Force, to get to combat in Korea. Best way to describe my tour in Korea is to call it a time of War and Truce. I will assert that in the haze of musing about times long past, my stories are true, but I am not quite sure about which battalion I was in, whether an event occurred in time of combat or of the truce, and on which side of the Imjin River I found myself.

*   *   *

Before Korea, however, all hands had to visit Pickle Meadow, the Cold Weather Training Center for the Marines in the Eastern Sierra, near Bridgeport, California. Elevation of that camp was about 7,000 feet with ranges up to 12,000; lots of snow; no frills. The presiding officer there was a veteran, a tough, seasoned leader, and the routine was a few days of living, communicating, eating, and moving as a unit in the cold and snow. A Marine had to carry his whole load on his own back, and the snow was so deep that travel was only possible in single file. I thought the crammed bus ride in the dark up and back from Camp Pendleton was the worst part. It was important training for replacements bound for the Korean winter, and Korea proved to be the coldest spot I have ever experienced.

95

*   *   *

I arrived at the headquarters battery of the 11th Marines, the field artillery regiment of the First Marine Division. We were stationed at the western end of the front, above Munsan but short of the Imjin River and not far from Panmunjom. I was made the R-2, as we termed it at that level, with responsibilities of overseeing targets, supervising a tricky business of counter-mortar response, and watching over a very idle antiaircraft battery. Keeping up the morale of unneeded troops sitting week after week on some hilltop was difficult. Their problems were different from those of other troops. The burdens of war are always unequal.

In the headquarters battery I had an impatient sense that I was not making much progress in my aspiration to get out from under. It was a staff assignment again, while my seniority appeared to allow me to command. I was scornful of a regimental officer, truly an inappropriate one for the FMF—he decreed that the rocks be painted white and armed sentries be ceremonially posted outside his tent. His address to subordinates was sometimes sarcastic, intervening in the fire direction tent with enlisted men involved in a mission. He would inspect to see if there were the proper number of rounds in cartridge belts, or when a busy man had taken his helmet off, ask him, "How do you like this steel-covered tent?" Sarcasm is just not the way to lead and inspire. Anyway, I had had much more combat time than he.

I would get myself up to the semi-permanent line of deep trenches in the hills, which constituted the front. Occasionally a forward observer could spot some indication of the enemy, but their trenches were probably much deeper than ours. We relied on aerial observation. We fired interdiction or harassing missions. There was one key, major, observation post alongside the road that led to North Korea. In a winter when electric generators were like gold and thus only little light at night, it was a shock to realize that some troops were bargaining for them with other units. One little

96

luxury spot (a foxhole?), contained a generator in order that the occupants might operate their electric blankets. On one visit I ran into some forward observers who I felt were not alert in their support of infantry patrols. I kicked them into better performance, although it was more a temporary inattentiveness rather than any big deal in the situation that day.

In general, throughout my tour the front had stabilized. Neither we nor the enemy were making aggressive moves. There was patrol activity, but as I later heard a Brit of their Commonwealth Division say, "We leave the bloody blighters alone, and they leave us alone." We were once visited by the brigadier commanding the artillery of that Commonwealth Division. He was a tall, impressive figure, as was his accompanying aide. They rode in a rather special jeep, which I am inclined to call the Rolls Royce of all jeeps. The brigadier affected a tremendous shepherd's staff, bigger than that of any bishop, and riding with them was his massive, tail-wagging dog. He judged this a quiet time, so they were all going for a swim in the Imjin. The British were our staunch allies, as of course were the troops of several other nations. They had provided Royal Marines in the earliest fighting and had committed the gallant Gloucestershire Regiment into fierce combat to stop the North Koreans. Tragically they lost their colors, symbol of a military unit's heart and soul. So years later when I resided in England, attending Oxford, it was most meaningful for me to attend Gloucester Cathedral, where this heroic regiment was memorialized.

At times one could really feel distressed at inactivity. An opportunity was offered me to take an R&R visit to Japan. I hung around Tokyo for a bit, but the sole remembered event was attending the famous Takarasuka show with all-female casting. I was embarrassed that the regimental commander's purpose for me was to pick up the special chinaware ordered for the regimental mess. It was not yet ready.

The regimental headquarters troops were kept partially busy, with lots of Korean labor help, in constructing a new regimental chapel. I note this because the chapel was dedicated to Saint Catherine, protector of travelers and, I am told, artillerymen. At its dedication we were visited and reviewed by Gen. Maxwell Taylor, commanding the Eighth Army. I was to serve very personally with him in time to come, but I never intruded upon him with mention of this first meeting, although my service with him when he became chairman of the Joint Chiefs of Staff under President Kennedy was intimate.

*　　*　　*

I had the rank of major now, so the regimental commander, knowing that sooner or later there would be an opening or need for a replacement, sent me on a tour of the four battalions. We now also had 155-millimeter howitzers, a step more potential up from what I had known in WW II. I visited about five days in each of the battalions, emplaced across the river. There was a different feel to life here across the river—not that there was any true increased danger, but now one would wear a steel helmet and could find himself within potential range of the enemy fire. Shortly after this indoctrination I was assigned as the commanding officer of 3/11, gratefully feeling released from staff duty. My tour in 3/11 was short because there soon arrived another lieutenant colonel to supplant me. However, I could say I commanded for a time in combat. The armistice was soon to come. Remembering, there were few important episodes to recount. In the cold we all had space heaters which were meant to be banked at night. Unfortunately we were careless about one of mine. Sort of embarrassing to explain about the resultant fire. I recall finally getting cement to set a good floor for our galley. But on Christmas Eve, no less, we found ourselves at the difficult task of rigging warming lanterns a few inches above the wet cement to dry it out. And, one night our much-needed shower tent lining was stolen, and by our allies, some South Kore-

98

ans from nearby. They were sometimes more of a hazard than the occasional, individual, enemy who sneaked into our perimeter from across the Imjin.

On a couple of occasions I had memorable, personal, meaningful encounters with naval officers serving with us. A red-headed, personable, lieutenant commander, Catholic chaplain, chatted with me, but casually mentioned that the Carthusian order of his church was special in that its members were bound not to eat together nor to speak to each other except on certain days. What then could he be doing here in Korea with Marines? His explanation was that he had been given a deliberate leave of absence for perhaps two years, freeing him from the obligation. Remarkable! And this. The naval service was well behind the army in acceptance and recognition of blacks. They were still only messmen in the navy. In the 11th Marines at this time I can only picture a single black, although we may have been sneaking ahead with integration. This sole black was in my battalion, and a Navy lieutenant, and our doctor. One evening we stood together in the moonlight, and I said to him, "I hope your people are beginning to get a better break with us now."

*　　*　　*

I was transferred somewhat before the armistice changed the intensity of the Korean War. We shot up most of our ammunition as 12:00 approached on the big night. In my next job as executive officer of 4/11 my c.o. decided that I would be a good one to select a new area for our howitzers on the south side of the river. Korea was a mass of rice paddies, and crops came to harvest three times a year. Unfortunately, I picked what looked like a simple meadow but in fact was an overgrown, abandoned rice field. We had a miserable time finding stable bases for our weapons. I am afraid I was the cause for much, laborious trucking of rock in order to keep our weapons from sinking down into the mud. The division declared that all hands should stir themselves out of stagnant, long-stabilized positions, so we trained at being mobile once again. These mild maneuvers were termed RSOPs, for "reconnaissance and selection of position." We even got down to Inchon and on board ships, just to renew training in what our business of amphibious warfare was all about.

Men were required to complete short hiking courses every day in order to restore fitness. One unit set up a circular course, but a couple of wise guys tried a shortcut across the circular route. Sure enough, disaster—there had been landmines emplaced in this area when it had been under enemy control. On the subject of landmines, they were a danger particularly threatening to the infantry. So when I sat on a board for awards and medals, I just could not approve a medal to one helicopter pilot. He had once, for a minute, on a given day, in a specific spot, merely set down in this vast theatre of combat, where there might have been a mine. Some Marines had to live day and night in areas where there was constant threat of them.

In some ways the truce was more strenuous than the war. We were not infantry stuck with the worst of jobs, but our troops had to spend hours picking up concertina wire and filling in old trenches. Now it was a time of raging heat, and I am sure many ignored the division order that all men had to keep their field jackets on even when laboring in the blazing sun. Korea was also about the hottest place I had ever known.

We had a crusty veteran, top sergeant whose time it was to return home. The c.o. decided that he should be awarded a letter of commendation or even a medal—although I reflect that medals only got awarded from Washington and HQMC. He had been shifted to the hospital ship at Inchon, so I was to take a helicopter shuttle to contact him. Before I flew out, however, some enlisted men (privates or corporals, subordinate to the top), told me that there had been poker games and that he was bailing out owing them money. So I was to chase him for a different purpose than giving him an award. On arriving on board *Jutlandia,* the converted royal yacht of Denmark, it was odd to enter by a double staircase into what?, the lobby or drawing room, of a hospital ship. I did not get my guys their money back, but I threatened him—no repayment meant no award and no release to return home.

*   *   *

There was one grand celebration, in June of 1953, that involved the entire British Commonwealth Division. The First Marine Division had been withdrawn well back, but doctrine prescribed that artillery is never placed in reserve. Accordingly we were now supporting the Commonwealth Division. The aggressive and fearless Turkish Brigade also supported the Brits. Once a Turkish patrol had heroically penetrated into a zone that was considered beyond proper objective as we negotiated a truce. They had taken a hilltop at the expense of several casualties. But 8th Army in Seoul had ordered no aggressive moves now, so after the fact, after their assault, the next morning when it was all over, the Turks were ordered to withdraw from the seized objective. It was much to their chagrin and temper.

The celebration was for the coronation of Queen Elizabeth and I cannot but remember that on the same day in a previous year in Tsingtao, China, I had attended the last birthday of King George VI. It would seem that this was a good day, the ceremonial birthday of the monarch, to get her crowned as well. It was the biggest beer bust of all time, although I have previously written that the USMC and Army Air Corps blast prior to Iwo Jima was the biggest. Featured were several friendly fistfights between Yanks and Limeys. A very dramatic show was that put on by the Turks dramatizing whirling sword fighting. It was almost too realistic.

The Turks were our neighbors then, but there occurred an incident that could hardly be thought of as friendly. On a very rainy night, four little bums, on the extra police duty as messmen which was usually handed out for mild misbehavior, stole the c.o.'s jeep. Next day we got a startling report that there had been a pretty frightful event in the Turks' zone.

Many Turk officers had welcomed assignment to Korea and combat. Some (of course not all) thought it particularly great that they could get repeated R&R jaunts to Japan, where they could find neat ladies and "hotsy" baths. Our neighbors now, copying this delight enjoyed in Japan, had set up a "hootchie," (a shack, call it their club) for rendezvous with available Korean females. I today remember that this was not the only kind of spot for such assignations. It was not uncommon to find ladies right out in the bushes plying their trade with U.S. Marines as well as with the Turks. The jeep load of our four certainly did not get away with anything of this nature that night, for the Turk officers had their treasure site well guarded. In fact, our four were intercepted by a Turk MP. One of them shot and killed him.

This is called murder. It was obligatory for the command involved to conduct what was known as a formal pre-trial investigation. As battalion exec I got the job. I was assisted in this inquiry by a pair of senior U.S. Army NCOs. They were designated CI, after Criminal Investigation, and I was lucky to have their assistance. I became a very busy individual. Follow me here: four accused Marines, lawyers, a misappropriated jeep, the rainy season, a murdered Turk MP, Korean whores, Turkish and Marine Corps witnesses, interpreters, jurisdiction complicated by U.S. Marine Corps personnel accused of offenses upon a Turkish Brigade, under the British Commonwealth Division, a part of the U.S. Eighth Army, under United Nations mandate. We had to travel daily for many miles, in convoy, in the rain, across the Imjin—with me, the four accused, their lawyers, interpreters, the jeep drivers, the poor devil of a sergeant who had to record pages and pages of verbatim testimony, and don't forget the mechanic who could start the generator to enable recording of the verbatim testimony.

After the formal pre-trial investigation, a general court-martial for murder would convene. The wheels of U.S. justice turn very slowly, especially when the charge is murder. The presence of Korean whores and Turkish witnesses had to be ensured. The CI investigation, my investigation, and the general court-martial all seemed a bit repetitious and unnecessary to the whores and the Turks. They wanted no part of all of this. The Turks were enraged at all Marines, Americans, and a petition had to go all the way back to the United Nations to delay their return home.

The division legal officer reported that I had done a perfect job. I was able to resist against assignment again to G-2, for this was pretty important stuff requiring my continuance in 4/11. It saved my job. Which one of the accused actually fired the fatal shot? Could they not have been acting in self-defense from the MP's challenge? They got off. Only misappropriation of the jeep could be hung on them.

Stateside and Vietnam

Assuming Command, 4th Bn, 10th Marines

On Parade, Camp Lejeune, North Carolina

Change Of Command, 3rd Bn, 10th Marines

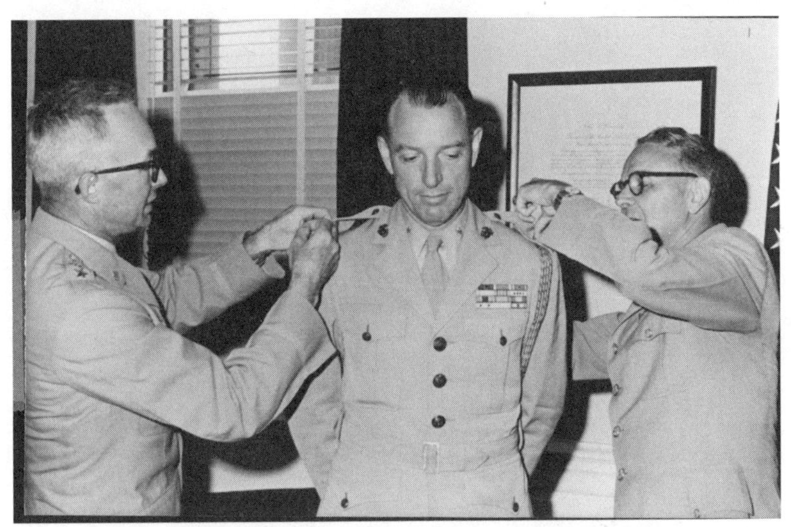

Generals Taylor and Goodpaster Pin Them On

Third Marine Division Bunker

Riding In A Helicopter

In Danang

Searching For Viet Cong, Or Finding Innocent Villagers

NINE
Taiwan, Early and Late

In the Far East for me there had first been mainland China. I also had my time of war and truce in Korea. The other, third, locale for my life in the Far East was Taiwan. I experienced that isle in several adventures—on a 1948 visit from Tsingtao with Admiral Badger, in 1953 and 1954 before and after my tour in Korea, and in my 1954–57 assignment as assistant naval attaché in Taipei.

*　　*　　*

I venture back to that voyage to Taiwan which ComNavWesPac undertook in late 1948. This kind of trip was sometimes termed "showing the flag," but the real purpose was to have a look at where Chiang K'ai-shek and the Nationalist, Kuomintang, regime might withdraw. Taiwan showed a very Japanese coloration at this time, they having been there for fifty years, since the Sino-Japanese War of 1895. The native Taiwanese were fully Chinese, however, and spoke the dialect of Fukien, opposite on the mainland. In fact over generations the historic function of Taiwan was to be an escape hatch, an overflow haven, after rebellion, famine, disease, floods, or political insurrection. And wave after wave of immigrants would drive their predecessors further out of the better, fertile, eastern lands. Ultimately the native aboriginal tribes had ended up in the mountainous, central spine of the island. The Japanese were never able to enter here, never even attempting to subjugate the aborigines. My personal, childhood in-

111

terest or connection was that I collected stamps. A rare and exciting find would be one from Formosa, land of head-hunters—purported cannibals.

I do not now attempt to give a lengthy account about events upon the island, because my thought is only to tell of how I experienced it in a personal way. *Eldorado,* our amphibious command ship docked in Keelung in the northeast corner of the island. Once upon a time Commodore Perry, in a diversion connected to his Opening of Japan, visited Keelung where his interest was the availability of coal essential in the dawning age of steam navigation. It was a bus or jeep trip from there up to the capital, Taipei. There was a minor, river entrance port, Tamsui, in the northwest. I find interesting, revealing, to comment that Tamsui means "fresh water." It was a rare spot where sailing ships in another age could call in order to fill their water casks. Taiwan's only true port lay in the south end, Kaohsiung.

Within the Keelung. Taipei, and Tamsui triangle there was a hilly, verdant, forested area known as Peitou. There were to be found great pits of steaming calcium and hot springs, whose waters might be funneled into homes and "hotsy" bathhouses. One such house was called "The Literary Inn," rather an inappropriate name for a good place for nude swimming and the other activity that went on there. It was said that when visiting Americans from Japan paid visits upon the ladies at the inn, Madame Chiang K'ai-shek had a report of their names on her desk by morning. On the subject of hilly areas, in the distant south of the island was the highest mountain in the empire of Japan. However, it was carried at several less feet than its true altitude so that Mount Fujiyama could be considered supreme.

The U.S. Embassy was establishing itself here in Taipei, and the biggest, most important edifice in town was the Japanese-built Ministry of National Defense. The rail system of Taiwan was impressive. In fact, China's first stretch of rail line and first locomotive, translated as a "fire cart," were said to have been built here.

The island had been called by foreigners, "Formosa," after its "discovery" supposedly by Portuguese. However, they had merely called there en route to Japan. The rambling, brick fort, adjoining the home of the British consul general overlooking Tamsui roadstead, had really been built by Spanish arriving from the Philippines. At this time it was utilized for penning up chickens. We were all glad to return from Taiwan back to Tsingtao just before Christmas, 1948.

*   *   *

I can call my 1953 and 1954 Taiwan–Korea–Taiwan adventures as sort of a sandwich. Brief tours of duty unrelated to field artillery, intelligence, and combat had brought me to Taiwan, both preceding Korea and before I could get home afterward. Following our cold weather indoctrination visit to Pickle Meadow, the next step was usually embarkation for duty with the First Marine Division, engaged with the North Koreans and those other, non-Taiwanese Chinese. However, I got a surprise assignment for temporary additional duty, as it was called, with the Troop Training Team, associated with the Navy Amphibious Command, based in Coronado, California.

The team was flown to southern Taiwan, this time to Taichung in the southern end of the island not far from Kaohsiung and the headquarters of the Chinese Navy and Marine Corps at the suburb of Tsoying. We were committed for a few weeks training of the Chinese Marine Corps. Some twenty of us, officers and NCOs, were billeted in what could be said to resemble a motel. Relative comfort and enough room for volleyball. The chow was so good and plentiful that after a bit of experimentation one would specify certain items or entrees to be left off the order. We would enthusiastically place an order such as, "One, no soup" or "Three, no dessert."

The purpose was to help train the fledgling Chinese Marines.

They would prove very highly capable, given their scarce equipment in amphibious vehicles, tanks and trucks. Incidentally most of these had been scoffed up at an abandonment, giveaway, departure sale, of U.S. Marines as they sailed from Tsingtao. We knew the efficient supply expert who saved much booty for Chiang, as "General West Point Wang." Lectures at Tsoying were given with the help of interpreters under tough conditions of high temperatures in simple shelters. A sandtable was employed usefully in order to illustrate the organization, loading, and ship-to-shore movement of an amphibious force. It never had to be proven, but the motivating cry of the regime in Taiwan in those years was, "Back to The Mainland." Some would contend that the Chinese Marines, with their intensive training and semi-permanent personnel lineup, perhaps equaled the readiness of regular USMC battalions on Okinawa, faced with yearly cycles of training and retraining as new troops spun in and out.

I do not now try to differentiate between my two, Troop Training Team, experiences in southern Taiwan. They were conducted under the general guidance of the U.S. Military Assistance Advisory Group. Our country has and probably continues to use such a command to assist an ally. That headquarters had little day-to-day contact with Tsoying's Chinese Navy and Marine Corps. We felt a bit removed from Taipei, the Ministry of National Defense, Chiang K'ai-shek's administration, and the MAAG. The USMC regulars on assignment in Tsoying, more importantly than we temporary TTT visitors, performed diligently in their training mission. It was a primitive and difficult atmosphere for the few U.S dependents on the scene. Some foreign missionaries shared the life here. School was conducted for children by correspondence courses. For high schoolers, the senior naval advisor had a plane with which he could fly students for their five-day school week back and forth from Baguio in the Philippines. And medical support was simple (in truth it was inadequate). I recall one gallant USAF doctor struggling to help his patients in a Chinese naval hospital. It was excruciating to watch one medical man tend serious cases. As for me, making this personal for a bit, I was hospitalized a short time for some minor business and was surprised that I had to buy, pay for in cash, my own drinking water.

One day in Kaohsiung I greeted Capt. Al Kilmartin, a navy captain whom I had earlier known in 1948 on the mainland in Tsingtao. He also was a Chinese linguist, was completing his assignment as captain of a USN vessel, and told me that he was next to return to Taiwan as U.S. naval attaché. Before setting forth on these Korean and Taiwanese overseas ventures, I had been promised by the personnel assignment desk that I was to return as assistant naval attaché under my friend. When I returned to HQMC, however, I discovered that there was a different lineup at work and that someone else was to get that sought-after billet. The officer in Taipei then holding it down was an aviator, for the reason that the office had an aircraft assigned to it. I knew that the said aircraft had been given up so was indignant that another with no background nor interest nor qualification should get that job. I had to fight a bit for it, but after a spell of briefings at the State Department, the Office of Naval Intelligence, and HQMC I got what I wanted.

The time was the height of the McCarthy era, the China Lobby, and the "Back to the Mainland" posturing. Just before leaving Korea I had watched prisoners of war choosing to return to Communist China, defiantly throwing off their clothes and cheering for Mao. But there were opposite numbers who cast their lot with the Republic of China. Many of them had tattoos on their arms to show their allegiance. Most memorable was, "Mao Tse-tung is a Turtle's Egg." The mythical turtle in oriental lore holds up the earth. The "egg" is what drops out of the turtle's bottom. So when I got to Taiwan it was not a complete surprise to discover occasional soldiers either still in uniform or holding down jobs as hotel doormen or bank guards—still displaying said tattoos.

*　*　*

Taiwan, in my post-Korea assignment as assistant naval attaché, was still building up as Chiang's nation in its smaller reincarnation. There were shortages of housing for Yanks, but I soon established a pleasant home. I cannot say that this tour was much of a military experience insofar as the U.S. was involved, but I certainly participated in naval affairs, State Department diplomatic events, the visits of politicians, recognition of the CIA presence, and the effort generally to support the Kuomintang cause. We lived well, were expected to employ the minimum of about four servants, played tennis and golf, and enjoyed the best of parties at the Grand Hotel. It was reportedly under Madame Chiang's personal management, the best accommodation in Taiwan.

I recall my Taipei home and an important, pleasant addition to my household. One day in the simple, English language periodical on which we depended for entertainment if not true news, there appeared an odd advertisement, "For Sale, lasateria." Was this maybe a misspelling of cafeteria? Was some restaurant for sale? Having known them on the mainland, I immediately recognized the availability of another Lhasa Apso, my special breed of dogs. Could it be a Lhasa Terrier? No cafeteria was for sale, and I quickly got in touch with the owner. He name was Allen Gan, and I can best describe him as sort of a latter-day Peter Lorre, the one-time movie actor. We became fast friends. Peter Lorre, I mean Allen Gan, was mild in manner, slight in stature. I wondered at times if he took the pipe. Under the Japanese, the Taiwanese were allowed little privilege, including higher education. But Allen was a medical doctor, a veterinarian, and a dentist. He described his father as a baron, head of a family that had held slaves. I suppose he exaggerated and that the slaves were merely the poorest of the poor given homes and a living at the lowest level of society.

Allen informed this assistant naval attaché of some fascinating facts. He told me of the practice of a Chinese ruler or warlord

116

to arrange for an orphan, for example, to be emplaced in Indo-China, Thailand, or Korea, there to be brought up, indoctrinated, and trained; and to emerge from that other society oriented in favor toward the Kuomintang. He gave me information on Koreans and Vietnamese who were actually Chinese and whose loyalty and support would go to Chiang. And once, with participation by the French charge d'affaires, an old acquaintance from Shanghai days, we visited an obscure port in the sparsely settled eastern coast of Taiwan. There we observed a French submarine secretly arriving as a link to Hanoi.

I was designated by the U.S. ambassador as the representative to attend the daily briefing of the top Chinese command at the Ministry of Defense. The MAAG also had its representation in attendance. I sat directly behind the highest officer in the Chinese hierarchy. Translators helped us foreigners to comprehend what was discussed or reported, but I cannot believe it was ever of great importance. That brings me to a general observation. Here was the attaché group of officers—we all had diplomatic passports and were accredited to the U.S. Embassy. But what is an intelligence officer, a G-2, meant to do in the first place? Well, let us say, find out things about the enemy. But who or what was the presumed enemy? Mao Tse-tung and his millions had taken over on the mainland. But for all our personnel, paperwork effort, and communications devices very little was ever uncovered in Taipei and Taiwan on what was happening on the mainland. Why then were we there? What was our purpose? The same might be said of State itself and the CIA. The latter had a large number of officers, but then their establishment in Hong Kong was said to be our largest intelligence office of all.

*   *   *

I enjoyed getting loose and roaming about Taiwan. Tsoying in the south was headquarters for the Chinese Navy and Marine

117

Corps, where I had friends and had served on the TTT training missions. It was natural to find there more to do and to think up something to report about our ally, than that enemy on the mainland. I got a little closer to the point of it all on a couple of trips I made to the offshore islands. The Republic of China continued to assert sovereignty on these islets, called the stepping-stones for the "Return," but they were pretty inconsequential. Matsu had no airfield and any landing by an old seaplane was a bit uncomfortable, but exciting. As an attaché I was a guest there, and I shared in the troops' diet of rice gruel and tea for breakfast and the barest morsel of some fish added to that same old rice at other meals. The MAAG thought they should supervise me on Matsu, but I declined their care. Other U.S. personnel on Matsu deemed the drinking water unsafe or at least distasteful, so they arranged to have the precious liquid laboriously flown in by seaplane or brought by Chinese naval amphibious craft. If they believed this to be some kind of sanitized or pure, bottled water, they were mistaken. I used to see the jugs being filled up by an ordinary public faucet on the grubby street near my home in Taipei.

Chinmen Island was a bigger island, and it supported a few thousand rural Fukienese in the outer harbor of Foochow. Nothing ever became of the blustering back and forth between the two sides. However, it was a good site for the transfer of goods by smugglers or pirates, going either way. I believe, too, that mail or other communications of real consequences went to and fro between Taiwan and Big China through this connection. For long spells there was the Chinmen Island Standoff. We fire on you with our artillery only on even days of the month, and you get to return fire on us on the odd. Most of it was bundles of propaganda leaflets, in any case.

Another destination for exploration was the Pescadores, a large number of small islets halfway across the Taiwan Strait. They had been termed thus by the Portuguese, but of the western powers experimenting there, the French were the most prominent.

Makung was the capital, and it boasted only the simplest of hotels, and maybe a movie theatre. But who knows how many movies, given only one generator for power? One lived on fish in the Pescadores. One of the loneliest souls I have ever encountered was a single, missionary lady, doing her best in this forlorn outpost. Probably just as lonely and barren was an isolated coral atoll known as Pratas. Here there was only a military and naval garrison. In the nearby Paracels there was a festering dispute over sovereignty, between the Chinese Nationalists, the Communist Peoples' Republic, the Philippines, and who else? They were the most barren, treeless, sun-blasted, wind-swept specks imaginable. But the prize was, someday, oil, to be found and exploited from below the waves. Once with my buddy, Harry, the assistant army attaché, we paid a call on forlorn Pratas Isle. It was about as big as a football gridiron. Not much to report.

*　　*　　*

I find I have always had an interest in law and justice as they are played out wherever I find myself. There were some episodes in Taiwan which were good examples of differences in what an American or a Chinese might expect. First, one of Generalissimo Chiang K'ai-shek's admirals had been sent to San Diego to pick up a destroyer for transfer to the Chinese Navy. He decided to cram it full with television sets, refrigerators, air conditioners, perhaps even an automobile or two. At court-martial time the Gimo's dictate was, "Let the punishment fit the crime." Sounds like Gilbert and Sullivan, does it not? Chinese law in this case looked at the case differently from what we are used to. Why bother to bring this offender to trial unless he should be guilty? The sole purpose was to determine the penalty.

During our tour there occurred a much more serious double-action, two-act drama. The MAAG chose its personnel with great care to ensure good relations in this naturally sensitive scene.

Sometimes an enlisted man could not be expected to have the patience and understanding of, say, a diplomat. A sergeant, with his wife and children, occupied an isolated home in the hills outside of Taipei. One evening his security and tranquility were devastated by the intrusion of a Peeping Tom. The sergeant's reaction was fatal recourse to his pistol. There ensued a general court-martial, for murder. The accused contended that it had been the very dead of night, and that he had been overwhelmed for the safety of his family. The court was transported to the scene at an equivalent moment of darkness to carefully evaluate such a defense by the accused. The Chinese authority had by then decided to mount a brilliant floodlight to prove that the scene had been far from dark. The court found him not guilty. It must have been self-defense. But to the Chinese—how could he not be guilty? Here lies the body, but the foreign spectators broke out in tremendous cheering as the verdict was announced. For this there was hell to pay.

Shortly afterward there were signs of the payback. Rallies were held. Protest placards had been prepared. Great indignation in the press. The U.S. ambassador was absent on a visit to Hong Kong. The highest Chinese authorities deliberately made themselves scarce, so that there could be no person nor official to whom to appeal over what followed. It was a full-force, planned riot. The embassy was attacked. The Marine guards were driven into what was a barricaded fortress. A humiliation had been countered with an assault. No serious casualties, but many bruised feelings. Proper apologies and explanations were exchanged. For me it was neither Korea nor Vietnam, to come, but one could say it was the next best thing.

TEN

Second Marine Division; Senior School, Quantico; and HQMC, G-1

I had had a rather heavy dose of the Far East by the time I returned from my long tour, three years on Taiwan as assistant naval attaché. The journey back in 1957 was memorable. My aspiration was for a meaningful command assignment in the Second Marine Division, Camp Lejeune, North Carolina. After my combat assignment in Korea and return from Taiwan, it was surely time for a "stateside" assignment. I hoped it wold not be just another spell in Washington, D.C.

I had an edifying, interesting journey from Taiwan after getting orders home. Permission was granted to proceed by what was known as circuitous routing, with travel time and a little excess leave thrown in. The routing stops by NATS (the Naval Air Transport System) were Manila, Saigon, Bangkok, Calcutta, New Delhi, Karachi—so now I'll pause in my account of making it to the 10th Marines, Second Marine Division, Camp Lejeune, North Carolina.

*　　*　　*

The most memorable tourist revelations for me in Manila were of General MacArthur's wartime headquarters and of a horrid little holding cell where the enemy had brutally held pathetic prisoners. Clark Field was our billet for just a couple of days be-

121

fore our next leg. Saigon we still thought of as Indochina. I had some acquaintances there, but the country was a French problem and no time for a tourist to look up pals. In Bangkok an assistant naval attaché counterpart showed me about, including the home of the fabled Jim Thompson, resurrector of the Thai silk industry who was to mysteriously vanish in the Cameroon Highlands of Malaysia on Easter Sunday, 1967. Calcutta was a poverty-stricken morass. New Delhi for me was priority to the cattle: all cows have right of way. Our visit overnight was at a magnificent hotel, but with no touch of the reality of those times. In Karachi I spotted a lone Mercedes Benz taxi, sort of interesting because I had ordered one in Hong Kong ahead of time, on recommendation of a Jesuit, missionary acquaintance in Taipei. It was for delivery, well, you will see.

From Karachi, next flight leg now run by the Air Force as MATS (or Military Air Transport System) was to be Dhahran, Saudi Arabia, or Cairo, Egypt. But a confrontation was going on between Israel and Egypt that said stay away from the Suez Canal. So we diverted to Khartoum, capital of Sudan. Khartoum was a lovely setting on the Upper Nile, but all I knew of it was that it had been the last stand for Chinese Gordon. I knew more about him as a warrior during the Taiping Rebellion in China than I did about him here in Khartoum. This NATS-MATS system of air travel, on which we were moving east out of Asia into Europe, seemed to have as an important task that of transporting out or returning to their homelands many foreign officers being trained for the several Military Advisory Assistance Groups the U.S. maintained throughout the world.

We emerged in Tripoli, Libya, where the most abiding picture for me today is of camels right in the downtown streets. We cut loose from dependence upon the U.S. air services and went BOAC, British Overseas Air Craft, which provided the link up to Rome via Malta. My personal logistic problem got a little burdensome now. I had committed to manhandling four heavy suitcases myself, which became known as my millstones. In Malta, which had a strong British touch, it was fascinating to view the ancient Christian catacombs and to remember Malta's importance as a crossroads of history. Arrival at Rome during the evening necessitated piling aboard the first available train rather than hanging around as tourists. We made Munich and after a pause boarded a superior German train to Stuttgart, home for Mercedes Benz. I was able to dump my millstones into a more convenient carrying arrangement. It was impressive, surprising, to observe that Mercedes Benz went out of its way to employ German war veterans who had lost arms or legs in the war—my war and theirs, though in different theatres. My wife and I subsequently enjoyed a self-drive, unimaginative, tour of lower Germany and the Italian Riviera. By now it was October and I could enjoy a swim in the Mediterranean and radio reception of the World Series over Armed Forces Radio. Going north we made Bremerhaven, where the U.S. Navy guys helped us and our Mercedes get on board a Military Sea Transport Service, MSTS, ship for stateside. Yes, it is about time that I get there, both in this account and in the very fact of returning from Taiwan.

*   *   *

Landing in Brooklyn Navy Yard at first I could not altogether shake off the years I had had in the Orient. I was picked up by Wally Doering, a USN pal, with whom I had served in Taiwan. He had served on the gunboat *Panay,* which had been assaulted, pre-war by the Japs on the Yangtze. I skipped through my old hometown, Scarsdale, and my old city, New York, for it had become about time to get back to being a real Marine. I had been out of the Fleet Marine Force for several years, so now as a Lt. Col. I aspired for assignment to the Second Marine Division, at Camp Lejeune, North Carolina. It was in December of the year, and I was not expected at Christmas time at HQMC. So I had to fight a bit to

123

get out of another tour at HQMC. My wife preferred the chance of resumption of life in our charming, converted barn home in Fairfax. Perhaps heretofore my omission of any reference to family hints of, well, a future split. I'll admit it now. This time she chose to linger in Fairfax rather than wait out with me for assignment of married officers' quarters at Camp Lejeune.

*   *   *

The leadership billets in the artillery regiment of the Second Marine Division were filled on my arrival around Christmas, but soon my predecessor as commanding officer of the 4th Battalion, 10th Marines, was relieved, giving me the opening to replace him. About my battalion, later, for first I must tell of the scene, the camp, and North Carolina. Sometimes we called it "Swamp Lejeune," for it was flat, flat as a pancake, bordering on the Intercoastal Waterway and the Atlantic itself. Occasionally groups could borrow the general's special fishing launch, cross the sandbar, and get out into the Gulf Stream for dolphins. Lots of land useless for civilian purposes, but not extensive enough for full, varied, artillery firing or maneuvering. Jacksonville was the community outside the main gate, primarily an overflow for the businesses, facilities, and recreational activities of Marines and their families. More interesting were Wilmington and Wrightsville Beach to the south, where one could find friends and weekend liberty. In the other direction were New Bern, an historic capital of North Carolina; Swansboro, which sticks in mind for its Sanitary Fish Market, meaning "no liquor allowed"; Morehead City, a minor harbor but available for amphibious embarkations; and Cherry Point, home to our USMC aviation buddies. Fascinating to me was nearby Pamlico Sound whose broad expanse but shallow waters the mail ferry had to cross for deliveries to Ocracoke Island. That little settlement was the end of the Outer Banks highway down from Kitty Hawk. In colonial times some of the Outer Banks were

124

forested, supported sheep and cattle, and the most isolated, lonely of homes and population.

I was an 08, signifying field artillery, and it was about time that I get back to that Military Occupational Specialty. It seemed that some things were conducted differently now, and in some ways I found peacetime presented more problems than wartime. The firing range was too small. We had to journey to the army's Fort Bragg for better training. At times we had to order yachts in the Intercoastal Waterway to hold it. We were exercising at direct fire, so better not venture in front of us for now. The land was so flat that a tower had been constructed for observation. Formerly I had been trained to conduct "Small T" or "Large T" fire. Too complex to explain now, but it required a mental agility greater than the simple "Up Four Hundred" or "Left One Hundred," that in this era could be directed from the tower. I knew very little about the weapons themselves, our howitzers, but good NCOs are what Marines depend upon. A leader tells a trained subordinate what to do, not how to do it.

I had very fine battery commanders, and the training in fire direction concentrated upon our lieutenants. One adventure concerned our pals, the aviators flying helicopters out of Cherry Point. Who commanded the helicopters while working with and for ground forces? When and where and with what loads do you go? One time in "Swamp Lejeune" a helicopter inadvertently dropped one of my howitzers from a good height. Down it went, somewhere in the bush and deep into the swampy soil. It was dropped by an aviator, but the Cherry Point Marines did not accept much responsibility for any search and discovery. My men had to hunt tediously for it for days, but it was never recovered. It had belonged to us, but we henceforth had a pretty good excuse for being one tube, minus. It would seem that since decisions over "if, when, where, or how" the helicopter is used in the first place, it appeared that the helicopter unit also had the search responsibility. It is not

exactly the same, but in Vietnam the parallel question was sometimes who commands a helicopter troop insertion, Ground or Air?

*　　*　　*

Aside from the basic field artillery training mission there
were a myriad of details, decisions, activities, and problems for a
commander. I discovered that 4/10 had a very high rate of enlisted
going AWOL, or overstaying leave either sloppily or intentionally
into AWOL status. I resorted to exhortation and appeal to pride at
formations. I had to lay it on their battery commanders. And I resorted to severity in handling these from now on. A problem
seemed to be that men would cram into a junk of a car and drive the
many miles and back for only short liberty periods in Washington,
D.C. Inevitably there were breakdowns or accidents on the road. A
more organized Saturday schedule would cut down D.C. trips.
Some did not care, so they were to earn a time in the brig. For every man in the brig his battery commander had to direct that an officer visit every day. A wasteful, distracting nuisance. Once I
questioned a rather pathetic, undereducated private from a broken
family in surely what was Appalachia, as to why he had stayed
AWOL. He replied, "They stole mah dawg!"

Leaving the level of dog-stealing, we one day uncovered a
more serious situation. An innocent private, returning from Jacksonville liberty on a bus, was confronted by a pair of fellow
Marines. They threatened him with knives, not demanding his
ready cash, but declaring that he must join their gang, pay them
dues and pay for the protection. One of the other requirements was
that one must defy a Staff NCO or deliberately disobey an order. It
turned out that this gang was being run by a baby-faced office
clerk. He was controlling who might request leave, who might
avoid the onerous tasks. I have to believe this gang had brought
their behavior into the Marines, my division, my battalion, as a
group from the slum of some eastern city. It was broken up by

126

courts-martial and transfers. One father, maybe with the same type of character or attitude, came in to wail about or protect his son. The gang had also spirited supplies of food out of the messhall, cowing or threatening a sergeant who afterward begged me to transfer him. He had for too long been in his speciality of mess sergeant and was now required to acquire more backbone. Good Marine Corps policy was that a unit takes care of its dirty linen. You just do not palm your troublemakers or weak sisters off onto some other outfit. In this case, however, what had to be done was to separate, break up, and transfer to the four winds the members of that gang.

Life in 4/10 was really not that nasty. We were competitive, especially against the infantry battalions, which generally had more salty, seasoned officers and NCOs. But my guys emerged on top or near there in all such activities as basketball, baseball, rifle qualification, pistol indoctrination, giving funds for the Red Cross, or wild enterprises such as donating to Belgium Flood Relief. There was a delicate line here. I was aware of a fellow, misguided commander who felt that you could buy his favor in return for higher contributions to charity campaigns. I was particularly gratified that one of my young, college-boy battery commanders won out in Close Order Drill competition over infantry units where many of the leaders were veteran, grizzled, tough officers commissioned from the ranks. One success had a double manifestation. It came time to fill a small Marine Corps quota to the U.S. Army's artillery course at Fort Sill. I sent off the first of my lieutenants with the encouragement that he do his very best. The full class was probably well over a hundred. On return, "How did you do?" His answer, "I was number one." This ain't all. A couple of months later, another session of the course, another candidate to fill the quota. I asked him, "Can you equal the performance of your buddy?" He, too, finished number one. They both were USMC regulars and hence were the choices for the extra schooling. That is not to minimize the excellence of the USMCR lieutenants in my outfit. I would try hard to integrate them as regulars, as we did also in getting men to reenlist. In the end, if the decision was to revert to civilian life, I proved pretty good in writing effective letters of recommendation for the best of law or business schools.

I made the most of this peacetime routine in a personal way in this organization training for combat, if and when. Another battalion was selected for commitment in the crisis in Lebanon. Remembered details are that the White House micromanaged to the degree that it be informed of how many rounds each Marine carried for his rifle; that many of Marines of that day did not know how to run their own mess in the field and units were decimated by dysentery; and that I, missing it all, was sent to sit on a promotion board at HQMC.

My captains and battery commanders performed magnificently over my three-year tour as commanding officer of two separate battalions. We cut that AWOL rate to zero. There were a couple of messy little episodes, however, involving officers, two of them being my classmates from our entering, Quantico, 9th Reserve Officers' Course. One, a major who had fallen behind for promotion, had probably served in another MOS, so had no field artillery experience or qualifications. We were engaged in firing exercises, on that tower platform, with all hands in field uniforms, carrying personal weapons, wearing steel helmets—you know, Training. My major, the battalion executive officer, showed up late and in his office-style, green uniform. It was an intolerable, embarrassing, failure in leadership, dignity, and example, during these peacetime years when the problems of morale and discipline were great. He was my classmate and friend, but I was saved from the direct necessity of personal action by a transfer, directed from above. There it is: that principle of taking care of your own, enlisted, dirty laundry, about which I have just proclaimed. But this time it was an officer who had to go.

The other officer, classmate, had been perched at the captain's level on that promotion ladder for some past reasons, and he, too, gave me a problem. Perhaps he was lazy, or just inattentive. His battery had routinely been given little leadership in form of schedules, plans, programs, inspections, even recreational activities, particularly on those Saturday mornings. As he appeared before me, and we had just begun to discuss the matter—he suffered a minor heart attack. He was soon retired. Not so good for him, but again I was saved from embarrassment over disciplining a friend.

My tour at CLNC was not just a series of problems in leadership and discipline. We had fun. The officers' club, particularly at Happy Hour, Friday afternoons, was a great occasion for being together. An old-timer told me, though, "You can't get into a good fist-fight now in the club, like you used to." There was a large post exchange for family needs, so one did not have to go off base. It was only a minor nuisance when we took our turn at the task of PX inventory—counting every tube of toothpaste to see that all was correct. The commissary took further care of our household feed requirements. I enjoyed ceremony and parades and admit that I needed a little instruction myself on carrying and saluting with the marmeluke sword. There were competitive athletics—poor golf for me, and tennis, fair enough. The CLNC hospital seemed little needed, but stood ready. Church services were conducted by the regimental or base chaplains, but Marines of that day did not display much spiritual need in the matter of attendance. For me I guess I missed more formal ritual and close companions with whom to share church. Maybe I was a smart-alec who felt security, but not yet, need of the Church.

*   *   *

One could plan for that inevitable time of retirement, by taking night courses at East Carolina College. With my background on China and Chinese, my instructor involved me in a weekend lecture-seminar in front of a large audience. Another participant was Owen Lattimore, the good and decent scholar and explorer of

129

Mongolia recovering from abysmal attack as an accused communist by Sen. Joe McCarthy. A third had the ridiculous title of "Lord" of so-and-so. He had been a "remittance man," sent because of his debts to China by family to get rid of him, had married a Chinese, had stayed on after Mao's victory, but scuttled back to the outside world after climbing out the second-story of a puny holding pen. China experts? I could think of nothing to say except to admire Lattimore's adventures in Mongolia. For my pains a retired officer out of the backwoods of rural Carolina ran me up to the commanding general of the division, as some sort of a dangerous commie. The general, who knew me well, just laughed.

*   *   *

I close out the Second Marine Division and Camp Lejeune, North Carolina on an episode of fortunate salvation of the career of one of my men. It gave me a proud feeling of achievement that may be surprising. In one of my firing batteries there was a Staff NCO, with probably eighteen-and-a-half years of service and an unblemished record. He was quiet, not flamboyant, kept to himself, and had supply or office duties rather than being out in front of subordinates in a leadership role. He one day suddenly went over the hill, AWOL, and had to be hunted down and brought back to base. He faced a court-martial and obviously had a tremendous lot to lose. His story was that his wife had been unfaithful and that he had had to do something about it.

Getting ready with the division legal officer for the action I was obliged to take, one of my lieutenants announced to me that he had been hiding a law degree which would have put him into legal assignment rather than duties he preferred with us 08s. Then, he added, "I am from Michigan and Michigan was the first state in the Union to take new recognition on a point of legal insanity." He told me that a revered chief justice of the Michigan Supreme Court, a personal friend of his family, had written a book entitled,

Anatomy of a Murder. It was being made into a movie at that very time—Jimmy Stewart, Lee Remick, Ben Gazzara.

Do I have your attention? The serendipity of this meeting, discovery, understanding, affects me still. The judge who steals the show in the movie was Judge Joseph N. Welch, and forgive me that I divert to remind you how he also had stolen the show in the Army-McCarthy hearings. "Until this moment, Senator, I think I had never gauged your cruelty or recklessness. . . . Have you no sense of decency, sir, at long last? Have you left no sense of decency?" Judge Welch stole both shows.

The point of *Anatomy of a Murder,* filmed in Michigan, was that an accused could know right from wrong but could not refrain from doing wrong. It might be more readily comprehended as the defense of "Irresistible Impulse." This was the theme of *Anatomy of a Murder.* It was gratifying that I, with the help of my Michigan lieutenant, the understanding division legal officer and compassionate commanding general, could dismiss the charges and save that sergeant's career and future.

*   *   *

There was next another Marine Corps Schools, Quantico,—or rather, a new, more grown-up, tested George Carrington was to return there in 1960 for another tour. With the WW II island campaigns of the Pacific, China, Korea, Taiwan, and heavy doses of Washington, D.C., and Camp Lejeune, North Carolina, behind me—it became time to "work my bolt" to get into the Senior Amphibious Warfare Course at Quantico. This was a prerequisite, sort of a must, if one was to have much of a future in the service. It hardly seemed to equate with the National War College and other service war colleges of the highest level, but who wanted a Marine who had not had another exposure at Quantico?

Sometimes we were unfair toward our fellow officers, instructors who had the misfortune of having to teach the likes of us.

"There but for the grace of God go I" could describe how some felt about instructor assignment. An important skill or technique was, however, imparted to instructors in what was termed "charm school." Rehearsing his speech or presentation, the victim was told no stuttering, no "ahs," or "ers." If he so faltered a big bell would be loudly clanged. Needless to say, the "you know" and the "I mean" repetitive expressions so often heard today in speech got themselves eliminated. Term them verbal pauses. Some of my college professors, with highly vaunted reputations and lecture courses, would have profited from this "charm school."

A playful, irreverent stunt was to close eyes and ears when a question might be posed on screen or verbally, to open them up when the "school solution" answer was revealed, and then mockingly to guess at what the question had been. Evaluating nuclear effects of an assumed aerial bomb—its detonating blast, subsequent fire, immediate radiation effect, hurricane effect of wind, and long range poisoning of places and persons—was horrific, but not a popular line of study or concern. One memory is what a bore it was impatiently to secure as Top Secret, perhaps four times a day, in a dial-secured box or locker, all the lesson material in re nukes. In a differing vein, an entertaining, but very unfair response was once made by a sleeping, lazy one of us, who when called upon by our instructor that day to comment on some matter, retorted, "Colonel, we have caucused here in the rear row about your question and selected my pal here to answer your question." That neighbor would have been sleeping as well.

However, there are serious, respectful comments on our experience at Marine Corps Schools. Despite the instinct to withhold credit for design of general staff organization and functioning from the Germans, surely they advanced the art of war. We would learn from them. Recalling for some, and explaining for others—there are four, specialist staff sections, which operate ideally under a managing and organizing chief of staff, while the general located on the top of the pyramid ideally just listens to all considerations and recommendations before rendering his decision. He is not to micromanage, like some presidents. He is not to order, "Tell me what I want to hear," like some politicians. The B'n-1, R-1, then, but S-1 or G-1 today, is the Personnel Officer. Are the troops trained, are there enough of them, properly distributed? The G-2 is the Intelligence Officer for the command. He confines himself to analysis of that enemy, not guessing what he might do, but what he is capable of doing. The Operations Officer, G-3, plans the operation, just how are we going to go about things. And we must heed the Logistics Officer, G-4, who reports on sufficiency of ammunition, trucks, or if the railroads can deliver in time.

A Marine must train and trust his subordinates, not only for their pride but to replace him if he should become a casualty. We must be clear and concise in giving orders. Let the mission and objective be *clear*. Such is achieved in a standardized and perfected five-paragraph combat order. We get there with a good staff study—look at the mission, present the problem, know the facts bearing on the problem, consider the options, make the recommendations, and decide. I had had experience in field artillery several times by the time of this return to Quantico. Controlling fire direction, intent that the rounds are going to get that enemy and none are going to fall short on our own, the G-3 runs the show. No one else can chat, talkers to the different batteries give readings or settings, and the horizontal and vertical control NCOs give their corrections. *There can be no confusion.* An occasion remembered is when a superior (maybe the regimental commander himself), interfered only in a minor way, but was addressed, "Colonel, get the hell out of my Fire Direction Center."

About clarity in speech and particularly in the military setting, think on this. We all know the answer to "Why does the chicken cross the road?" Are you quick and sure if asked "Why did they bury the left-legged soldier on the right side of the hill?" (Answer, just in case: He was dead.) It might be thought unnecessary, aggravating, confusing, or silly to insist at an inspection of the ranks on a proper answer to "Do you know your rifle number?" He being questioned is not to blurt out numbers, merely a simple, "Yes, sir." Expanding on this, try answering most questions with "Yes," "No," or "I don't know, but I'll try and find out, sir."

Finally, we often hear, "Let me make one thing perfectly clear," when the intent might possibly be just to argue, delay, or alter. Consider the martinet, drilling a column of soldiers approaching a cliff, who fails to command, "To the rear, march." At the disastrous result he can only declaim to his well-trained, obedient troops: "Don't do what I say, do what I mean!" At Marine Corps Schools we were taught to be clear and unambiguous. In those years of the Cold War, a derisive rejection of students' clumsy or inadequate plans could be, "Does Minsk fall?"

*   *   *

Overlaying in time while I was a student in the Senior Amphibious Warfare course at Quantico, I was involved in a completely different matter of school or schooling. I was taking night-school graduate courses at American University. Someday my Marine Corps days would be over—so get ready for a retirement career; perhaps teaching? The emphasis for the M.A. degree at American was upon that of my own country. I had had a good exposure to European history and had become acquainted with Chinese and Japanese history. So a couple of nights a week I would make a flying stop for dinner at my Fairfax home, steam by Robert Kennedy's home, Hickory Hill, and make it into D.C. for those class sessions. I had a passion for geography and history, so this insurance for some sort of retirement occupation seemed like a good fit. I particularly profited from the courses in American history, conducted by a respected professor, but with an attitudinal response different from mine. He had been a conscientious objector in WW II. We got on well together.

* * *

When the time came for my thesis my thing was the Chinese island of Formosa—yes, Taiwan. Another teacher in Asian studies was Ralph Powell, Marine Corps veteran wounded on Peleliu. I had known him in California at Berkeley language school. Ralph had suffered too many wounds to continue his Marine Corps career, but was now coincidentally encountered wearing his Ph.D. robe from Harvard. In my heart of hearts I hoped someday to achieve something similar. On graduation day in 1964, I would surprise my boss Gen. Maxwell Taylor, announcing that I had a date with his boss. President JFK made a memorable American University address at the ceremony that day. I have remembered another respected achiever that day, Sen. Robert Byrd, whom we watched get his earned—not honorary—law degree. He is still on the job as I write, a great and respected figure in the Senate.

* * *

After my Senior School course at Marine Corps Schools, Quantico, I was assigned again in 1961 to HQMC, this time to G-1. This was a break for a guy with a home in Fairfax and an aspiration to continue the night school courses at American University. G-1 of course was important. The section, under my old WW II commander (now Lt. Gen.) Al Bowser, planned personnel growth, assignments, quotas, and promotions. I wish I could always be cheerful, enthusiastic, and positive in all the matters in which Marines get involved, but again I had to regard my assignment as pointless. I was at a desk in G-1, termed Mobilization Planning. This was for the personnel considerations when and if WW III were to break out, the reserves called up, and thousands of new augmenting troops recruited, trained, and brought to duty. Camp Lejeune, North Carolina, home of the Second Marine Division, for example, would experience great expansion. When these numbers should soar, can you believe it?, I was to be ready with

135

how many new plumbers, electricians, carpenters, firemen, school teachers for dependent children, and mechanics the base might need.

Not much better was my selection as the victim to attend Pentagon meetings of the Joint Nomenclature Board. Here representatives from all the services sat to determine how military items, objects, subjects, persons, should be given titles or named. It was scornfully termed the "Changing Happy to Glad Board." Some of the other services put general or flag officers on this assignment. However, it was just impossible to take this business seriously in view of what was transpiring in the outside world.

I was assigned for just a short time to a promotion board for the selection of the first, post-war enlisted Marines to the important rank of warrant officer. There were spaces for only a precious few. The senior NCOs of the Marine Corps then were all battle-tested, loyal, highly qualified candidates. Many, many, deserved the promotions. We on the board were subjected to that old nemesis which I had experienced years before, Command Influence. "Promote my guy" was the message, which most of us ignored. On one occasion the reviewer for a particular candidate in this most competitive selection process, all board members being unable to review all cases—announced, "Gentleman, Mr. Green is black." He was the first ever to be honored by selection to the rank. It was of course deserved and he, outstanding, but this Marine Corps promotion board included some who felt that important, racial information had been unfairly withheld from them.

*   *   *

I was again in residence in my attractive barn home in Fairfax. Having two automobiles to a family was a bit of a luxury, so most of us enjoyed the camaraderie of car-pooling for the commute. Fairfax certainly was a convenient spot for one's job in either Quantico or HQMC. I was busy a couple of nights a week at school at American University, not much coloration to this activity, but we all would have to face retirement someday. I again enjoyed the Pentagon Athletic Club, good for volleyball and a sandwich lunch. As a Giants fan I had watched on TV there as Bobby Thomson hit the miracle homerun which beat the Dodgers in 1951. I joined the Army–Navy Country Club, good for noon-hour tennis. However, a total of four bus transfers to get there and back certainly extended that noon hour. I found myself at such an impasse for meaningful work that I could have asked for a transfer from my old boss. Lt. Gen. Al Bowser, G-1, under whom I had served on Guam and Iwo Jima. On one occasion I boldly just sneaked out to watch the Washington Senators play a day game—and another time and worse, I decided that I'd just bail out to attend a theatre matinee.

I must leave HQMC on a more positive note. It is not right that I should complain or criticize. I was dispatched to oversee training of reserve units at Camp Lejeune. I was able to assist particularly with field artillery batteries or battalions. As I came in from the firing range one day I met a representative from the base who told me that I had been selected for promotion to full colonel. It was not to take effect right away, but it was of consequence in the next step of my career.

Retirement Parade

A Brit And A Yank; Colonels And Cousins

My Wife, Dogs, Church, And Oxford Gown

FOREIGNERS IN FORMOSA
1841—1874

George Williams Carrington

My Oxford Achievement

The Marine Military Academy

Photo by Lydia Clarke Heston.

Really Retired

ELEVEN

Pentagon for JCS; Coronado, California; and Danang, Vietnam

JCS, just a few initials; but as Joint Chiefs of Staff they of course stand for the summa, the top level of the U.S. military. I had a surprising landing therein, and indeed it climaxed my career, even though it was peacetime, not war. I had been assigned to that dead end, Mobilization Planning, in the G-1 Section of HQMC. Reading the newspaper and getting away for noon-hour volleyball at the Pentagon, or tennis at the Army-Navy Country Club, were my solutions. I should have recommended a change to the Table of Organization of the section or begged for a transfer from the G-1, my boss there. Lt. Gen. Alpha Bowser who had been my field artillery battalion commander on Guam and Iwo Jima in WW II. One day I was summoned to the commandant's office. He was gruff, no-nonsense, Gen. David Shoup, our heroic leader at the assault of Tarawa. I interject one about General Shoup. He was once debating with a counterpart colonel who had been talking up his tough action in Korea. He ventured a comparison between his fight and that at Tarawa. The Shoup retort, "Yeah, but that was defensive combat." On the day I was summoned, the general merely said, "Get over there, and don't let me hear anything about you."

He was referring to the Pentagon, where I was bound as aide to the chairman of the Joint Chiefs of Staff. President JFK had suffered the humiliation of the Bay of Pigs. There was to be a clean sweep of leaders in our military hierarchy, and the new group was to be led by Gen. Maxwell D. Taylor as chairman. The general's record and career were impressive. He had been a Japanese language student, had instructed at West Point, headed the 101st Airborne Division in Normandy, led the Eighth Army in Korea, commanded in Berlin, and had been chief of staff of the U.S. Army. He had retired in protest over policy and inadequate support to the military, been active in reorganization of the Mexican telephone system, and worked on Lincoln Center in New York with John D. Rockefeller, III.

The billet in his office was for a Lt. Col., but the odd, special point was that the appointee had to be a tennis player. This was the chic activity in Washington, so my name had been sent over—not that I was Wimbledon material, but because the move was conveniently just across the street. I was to be the only Marine in the office, the other services contributing many more numbers and much more rank. It was a rarified atmosphere, and I certainly welcomed the transfer. About this business of staff assignment to the general—he was to joke with me, "I am chairman, but you are the only one I command." There was an initial period of an inter-regnum. General Taylor had his offices in the Old State Building, next to the White House, assembling his team of officers before the actual move to the Pentagon. He was actually away on one of his many investigation visits to Vietnam when I arrived, so I passed acceptance muster by his exec. The delay in Old State appeared to be sort of a minuet—stay away from the old, Bay of Pigs-tainted lineup, before becoming that new broom in charge of the sweep at the Pentagon.

I felt like a hot shot when we actually moved across the river. Suddenly I had the best parking slot for the whole Pentagon. The general allowed me his own space, since anyway he had two limousines, two chauffeurs, and parking in the basement. The different surroundings in which I found myself, different from those of my previous Washington assignment, intrigued me. The Pentagon itself had been completed just prior to the war, but I had known this ground long before. My Pops and I had experimented with my first, sightseeing and ride in an airplane at the field on the bank of the Potomac here.

The inner ring of the building, but maybe pentagons cannot contain rings, was a pleasant sandwich-lunch spot. The mall was convenient for taking care of minor services or shopping needs, but higher brass seldom ventured there. Today, but not in that time, one could catch the subway over to D.C., the big city. There were the sickbay, the cafeteria for the large Pentagon population, and especially the Pentagon Athletic Club. I was much too busy now to enjoy it. A tunnel led to Fort Myer, where the general lived but where I declined quarters. I still had that home in Fairfax Courthouse, via that long commute, in a car-pool, along Columbia Turnpike, through Bailey's Crossroads, and off the (General) Braddock Road. Fort Myer had tennis courts, so that is where I found myself needed usually on late Saturday afternoons. My Seventh Day of the week seemed only to allow time for church and a tedious job of mowing a big lawn.

I had always to be ready for the general's sudden and unexpected bursts into exercise. Was it really the need to relax and get away from it all that would lead him suddenly to leave the building on foot, without his cap, for a walk—down toward the Potomac, into Arlington Cemetery, about the grounds of Fort Myer? I could never be sure, but I had to alert the driver to pick us up at the presumed termination point, to bring along the general's cap, and to hurry to catch up to him. We were the only two in the chairman's office to wear the uniform daily. I had to get used to fellow officers all about me, but in civvies, unlike my previous HQMC tours. The walks together were a privilege. The chairman of the JCS was not a chatty conversationalist, but he allowed some rare, intimate exchanges with me—personal, history, travel, amusing observations, his problems.

The doors to the chairman's office were on the ground floor at that section of the Pentagon on the outside ring and just off the mall entrance, with my lucky parking space. The several doors were unmarked so they would not be known to any unauthorized nut that might try to enter. I sat in what I'll call a vestibule, but it was truly a small room, along with General Taylor's primary, military secretary. Across the hall were the social secretary, a lady brought along from his retirement life, and the chairman's galley and mess. The general early on told me, "My time is my money, and I don't let anyone steal from me!" That meant he would send over his luncheon order ahead of time, so No Waiting, Comparably, his habit was never to carry any money or keys.

On trips I would make certain that the bills or tips got paid. I carried a key to the elevator leading to the basement where that driver and limousine always stood ready for the next call. The destination was usually the State Department or the White House. Often General Taylor would meet Secretary of Defense McNamara on a joint summons to the president, or when they closed shop at the end of the day. Riding the elevator with them, there were snatches of small talk that one could not help overhearing. Once, Max or Mac, holding a dispatch from Vietnam, from General Harkins or Ambassador Lodge, quoted from it, "This coup is dead." And in the limousine, me in the front seat, the general once said, "You know, there are only three things in life that a man really needs—a good book, a bottle of Scotch, and tennis racquet." I do not remember who said this next one to whom, but in another political or philosophical musing, one of them said, "You know, there is a course, trend, direction, to American political life that does not change just because a president, an administration, or a preponderance in the Congress changes to or from Democratic or Republican. Things just settle down at the center position."

Within the chairman's office General Taylor lined up his selection of competent, dedicated, soldiers and sailors. I pay special tribute to two of them, coming up with my own measure of what was important. Gen. Andrew Goodpaster had been President Eisenhower's military aide in the White House, had headed the

Eighth Division of the Seventh Army, and was to command NATO, but best in my book is that the army later assigned him to West Point when that institution had had some trouble. And Gen. Bernard Rogers, who had been a Rhodes scholar at Oxford at the start of his career, impressed me when I heard how he loyally went out of his way annually to honor an elderly British general, Jumbo Goschen, who was to become my friend in England. The chairman's personal staff were to be distinguished from the Joint Staff itself. There were lots of papers to push, and above all, we had to be alert and timely in competition with JFK's White House staffers who might regard us military as stuffy and slow. It's basic to say that the best advice or contingency plan is not worth a penny, if it is not available in time. The general never let us forget this.

* * *

The Joint Staff itself was there, close, energetic, and resourceful. The particular kick at that time was called counterinsurgency, and there were plenty of trouble spots where it might apply. The brothers Kennedy demanded performance here, and the Pentagon effort was guided by Marine Corps Gen. Victor Krulak. Being from the same service as he, I admit that I made efforts to inform him what particular items were located on the chairman's agenda on a given day. I trod a narrow line here: I could not be disloyal to my number one boss, but there was nothing wrong about letting General Krulak know what was on the front burner. General Taylor, when he could not get to the matter right away, would mark my papers, "See me." I would sort out what I adjudged the first priority for those wanting to meet and talk personally.

All sorts of visitors clamored to see the chairman. An early experience was with a Central Intelligence Agency officer who had had big responsibilities during the Bay of Pigs fiasco. General Taylor and the attorney general—we all remember that it was Bobby Kennedy in that seat—had investigated the Bay of Pigs.

The CIA man wanted to know or correct the investigation as to his personal reputation or involvement. The stunt was not to let him in the door. General Taylor could or would not want to be known as a stonewall to the plea. Neither did he give me a direct order to forestall any visit. But I understood how I was to function. The principle was what could be called Deniability. One could explain it, "Do not tell me what I do not want to know." A midwestern congressman was once very intent on getting the general to make a special appearance, a special speech, in his home district—for his purposes, not for the general's benefit. There was application through secretaries, he involved me directly in his plan, and finally he ran me up to General Taylor. He showed me a scowl and, "What's this I hear about you giving representative so-and-so a hard time?" But then he broke into a pleasant smile.

I intercepted or helped with all sorts of visitors. Lord Louis, Admiral Mountbatten, called. Certain discussion was high-level and secret, but the superficial or secondary purpose was an historical question involved in the Official Secrets Act. Once a senator was hung up by the disappearance of his limousine so, meeting him in the hall, I loaned him the chairman's car and driver. I caught a little, temporary, flak on this, but we all knew I had done right. A lonely, elderly, naval captain once showed up at the mall entrance, seemingly impatient and confused. He actually did not want to see General Taylor, so I was proud to guide Samuel Eliot Morison to the Army Historical Division for his continuing research.

Chiang Ch'ing-kuo, the son of Chiang K'ai-shek, visited, and I was able to make the chairman's team look good by some minor social interpreting. General Taylor prided himself on his languages, having long before been a language student in Japan. He had taught French at West Point, had spoken German during his commandant time in Berlin, and was still interested in keeping up on his Korean. A researcher on Nomonhan, the 1930's battle between the Japs and Russians, once appeared, knowing of the general's familiarity with Japanese language and history. It was too busy a time, so I had to shortstop him. My point in including this seeming inconsequential meeting is that when I became close to retirement, he employed me to teach a graduate course at San Diego State about my China, not his Japan.

We had a meeting with Henry Cabot Lodge. He later was appointed ambassador to Vietnam, but at this time had hit a stonewall in his political ambitions in Massachusetts. He called on the chairman, whom Lodge remembered as the former chief of staff of the Army. He surely counted on General Taylor as perhaps influential in helping him. He sought to come on active duty as a major general in the reserves. His request was not met, but it might have been a sort of precursor to his services being picked up as ambassador to Vietnam.

And we had another visitor, pleasant but not so important, James Van Alen, a prominent, socialite resident of Newport, Rhode Island. He might have had personal acquaintance with the general. Or perhaps he was just taking the initiative in approaching another tennis devotee on the subject of his own tennis objective. He had thought up a new method for breaking the frequent six-to-six ties in a tennis set. Fans will know it. All employ it today. I do not try to explain, but it was a good way to separate winning from losing. I apologetically remind that I had come aboard because the commandant of the Marine Corps had assigned me across the river—because of that racquet game. And I had previously known Jimmie Van Alen on the clay courts of Marion, Massachusetts, my boyhood summer home.

John D. Rockefeller, II, the general's associate from his days at the Lincoln Center project, arrived at Washington National Airport, where I picked him up to be a houseguest at Fort Myer's Number One quarters. Again apologetically I explain that I was also able to recognize and be personal with him. As a teenager I had known him and Mrs. Rockefeller at their tennis game and in their sailboat—again referring to that sheltered life I had escaped in Marion. Their son Jay, today a respected senator from West Virginia, later also visited. He wanted his father's friend to advise him—should he get in the service or go Peace Corps? It is understandable that he took the latter course, where he did important service.

Teddy White, the noted author of *Thunder Out of China,* was now researching background on another of his *Making of the President* series. He sought an inspection of the scene, the Gold Room, inner preserve of the Joint Chiefs where they debated the important military crises of President Kennedy's term. I inherited the mission of escorting him there, but also learned just in time that I had better see if the coast was clear of some other visitors. It happened that the messmen who were serving coffee in the Gold Room, had been running or participating in a, or the, Numbers Game. Not too good a security standard at this summit of the American military. I had to make sure that the FBI was clear of the premises before Teddy White looked into things.

*   *   *

A spectacular couple of moments for me occurred at a time of the assassination of the president. General Taylor had locked his door and was napping, when Secretary McNamara demanded of me that the general be put on the phone. Truly before I could act, the secretary came pounding down the stairs—I remember his office as two flights directly above ours. From later reporting I learned that full knowledge of the tragedy was not released just then, but I recall Secretary McNamara hissing, "He's dead." The JCS put the Strategic Air Command on highest alert. At the time of another crisis, I confirm that, when our highest military was assembling in the Gold Room, a reconnaissance aircraft in Alaska had mistakenly ventured out of bounds, perhaps threatening the Soviets. At the confused, crowded scene, Secretary McNamara, recognizing my face before others, told me, "Tell the Russians it's

152

innocent." I sped down the corridor to where the Red Phone to Moscow was manned, the weight of the world on my shoulders. Of course, good officers on the scene had immediately taken action, said the right words. Good soldiers and sailors know what to do. They do not wait to be told.

Then there came the funeral. While the general was just another in the national and international assembly for that solemn ceremony, I was told to scare up sandwiches for him and General LeMay, Chief of Staff of the Air Force, for what came next, now the dramatic ride in the limousine over to Arlington Cemetery. Have a try at that job, at that time. Now the two generals were importantly conspicuous leading the procession to Arlington, me in the front seat. I was in my blues with the aiguillette rope of aide, facing all manner of cameras and spectators. Generals Taylor and LeMay bent way down in the back seat, munching their sandwiches and avoiding the gaze of outsiders. Their conversation, probably in awkwardness at this affecting moment of national tragedy, was amazingly prosaic. Max wanted to know if Curt was really serious in his enthusiasm for conducting motorcar racing on Air Force runways. And Curt challenged Max with something like, "Did you really man that baloney I heard in our last meeting in the Gold Room?"

*　　*　　*

We made sudden and important trips to Saigon in those years. Since I've mentioned the tennis racquet, I'd better tell this story. I was surprised to be summoned one morning for a game hastily arranged—General Taylor, the important Vietnamese leader "Big Minh," a colonel from the MAAG, and this aide to the chairman. Duong Van Minh was our big hope to liberate, reform, to turn around the political and military fortunes of South Vietnam. Robert McNamara was present, pretending great interest in the game, but inappropriately clad in his dark suit. He had to shed his coat and tie and roll up his sleeves in the stifling heat. At a changeover between sets General Taylor and Secretary McNamara attempted to isolate Minh for private talk. I was instructed, detailed, to try to keep a particular Vietnamese spectator, very innocuous in appearance, apart from this discussion. The true purpose here was to bring up the matter of a plan to change the regime of brothers Diem and Nhu. There was no way I could keep that very interested agent away. Perhaps the matter could be taken up with Minh another time, but George Carrington could not be of help here at this tennis match.

On matters of a different direction than Vietnam, NATO impelled us to Europe. I immodestly say that I did more than just open and shut the limousine door or carry the tennis racquet on these trips. Getting the ship underway, or now I should say boarding our flights for Europe, meant planning with the pilot, Lt. Col. Fred Rohde, USAF, who moved us on "Redford's Revenge." It was a slow propeller-driven, holdover from the admiral's, former CJCS, struggles with the air force, but it was true luxury. The chairman had a suite aft, eight staffers had most comfortable seats and full, seven-foot bunks, and the crew's galley operation was always outstanding. The air force allowed liquor on board, unlike the navy still bound by Josephus Daniel's prohibition. These comfortable flights differed from Secretary McNamara's on the stark, ordinary aircraft for his flights to Vietnam—lest he got flak over too much luxury in these gathering years of antiwar protest.

*　　*　　*

We would go to the NATO meetings in Paris in mid-December, crossing the Atlantic with optional stops in Bermuda and the Azores, in our prop job but in the jet age. After the serious matter had been concluded we once laid over for a 24-hour period of relaxation at Avignon's finest country inn, an occasion for a superior tour by a French professor and a magnificent gour-

154

met dinner. Spain, Granada, was a wonderful stop, where we were entertained at dinner and with music across the valley where the gypsies still reigned. Germany was scheduled, with an opportunity to make Garmisch-Partenkirchen. In Salzburg we visited Mozart's home. Rome was not on our return itinerary, but when pilot Fred made a midnight, surprise-to-the-general, stop there, he was angered and directed an immediate new takeoff. To avoid a dinner invitation he had directed too early a departure for next destination. That was Las Palmas, Gran Canaria, and now we had to circle, delay, and kill time because the relaxed American consul general was not used to meeting such early arrivals.

Athens, Teheran, Ankara, Islamabad, and New Delhi were our stops on a CENTO trip. In Athens I was occupied with more than just duties as an aide, becoming the recorder for discussions and decisions for the Joint Staff at home. We were required to survey where there was taking place an international Boy Scout jamboree. This was on the very ground of Marathon, where a massive, circular antenna system was contemplated for talking with submerged submarines. At Ankara my best recollection is of a show put on by the Turkish military, of strongmen, acrobats and wrestlers. In Iran the Shah's military leader wanted to discuss a plan that nuclear landmines be emplaced in the mountain passes for possible Russian moves south. In Pakistan the senior general presented himself in meticulous uniform, mentioning that he had a haircut every day. But he was due for a scolding from General Taylor for a little inattention to what the U.S. was doing for his country with respect to military aid. Nehru greeted us in Delhi, giving all roses. We visited in the east, in the valley of the Brahmaputra, where the Chinese had threatened incursion over the disputed McMahon Line and down into the lowlands of India. They were correct in their interpretation of the proper survey boundary in this crisis, to Nehru's embarrassment, and perhaps leading to the finish of his active career.

I leave mention of Switzerland to the last. We arrived exhausted. Waiting for the general was a summons from President Lyndon Johnson. It meant immediate return home and General Taylor's shift from CJCS to ambassador to Vietnam. Flying home over Portugal, I closely observed our path in my passion for geography and history. It was over the very point of departure from Europe, Sagres, where Henry the Navigator had built his observatory and explorers departed for their discoveries. I was to continue for a couple of months as aide to General Taylor's successor, Gen. Earle Wheeler. However, I knew I could and should move it along, so requested reassignment. I did not get what I ambitiously wanted, but it started me on the track that eventually got me to Vietnam.

*   *   *

My way stations, before and after Vietnam, just as Taiwan had been for my Korean tour—were in California. Specifically I went and returned by Coronado, the amphibious training center for the Navy and Marine Corps. This time I was assigned to the Landing Force Training Unit, where I was made the Inspector, with an energetic and competent Assistant Inspector, Lt. Col. James Blakely, but practically nothing to do. It felt like a big comedown from being aide to the chairman of the Joint Chiefs of Staff.

In time I accepted Coronado as a pleasant duty station. I had left the serious, heavy atmosphere of the Pentagon and could enjoy association once again with my buddies in the naval service. Coronado itself, with its historic hotel and the charming ferry connection to San Diego, was a dream community. North Island, where naval aviation of the Pacific was primarily based, had ships, planes, clubs, commissary, post exchange, golf, and tennis. San Diego was the best of California. I resided in a condo apartment in Chula Vista, from which one commuted over the strand, the beautiful stretch of sand south of Coronado. I had, of course, traveled to

156

Southern California before, a memorable time having been when I had driven a car there through the Imperial Valley. Being in Coronado brought back memory of my earliest days as a Marine, in a field artillery battalion firing into the empty desert near that fascinating Salton Sea. This time the scene was not desert, but dramatic San Diego Bay and the Pacific Ocean.

The Landing Force Training Unit actually was a school where U.S. and foreign officers were instructed in the techniques of amphibious warfare. There were a few European officers, but I fear some were overage with little true reason for assignment and maybe taking temporary reduction in rank in order to fit in. At the other end of the scale was a lone, quiet, lieutenant from Indonesia. One wonders at the reason for his assignment. LFTU also dispatched teams to the Far East for training of army units in Japan and Okinawa, and for the Chinese Marine Corps on Taiwan. I had taken part before in that training on Taiwan.

Alongside us the navy ran their courses, giving particular effort to a school for the Vietnamese language. From my experience with Chinese I just felt that there was little that could be taught for useful purpose in such short time, but our nation had to try—with regard to Vietnam. Naval gunfire support for Marines had been a traditionally important element of assault and development of a beachhead. The naval gunfire school and courses were the responsibility of several of my old associates from field artillery. We taught and demonstrated the ship-to-shore movement. There was instruction on how to combat load. As well, the navy conducted instruction on the beach for Navy SEALs.

As the Inspector for LFTU I was in a billet not a part of the table of organization. When we had our yearly visit from an inspection team from HQMC, they did all the inspecting anyway. I had no responsibilities in the classroom and I was idle in the headquarters building. I felt great sympathy for my assistant, Jim Blakely, who had had a series of bad assignments and had been hung up sick after his last training mission to Indonesia. It is an idle boast now—but a very good deed I did at LFTU and what is remembered today is that I wrote him up, praising him to the heavens, in an unequaled, two-page fitness report, making sure he would get his promotion.

*　　*　　*

So I purposefully sought diversions and preoccupations while at Coronado. It was a surprise one day (because I do not know how he looked me up) to be contacted by a faculty member of San Diego State. His specialty was Japan, but the need was for someone to teach a graduate course in Chinese history, or rather the story of the 19th century foreigners in China and Taiwan. I undertook this "moonlighting," as it was called. It was strenuous to instruct for three hours, although on only one night a week, and disappointing to wonder who were my students sitting before me.

A graduate course, with most hardly ever having even thought before of China? I was proud of two students, ashamed of one. A lad from Iran had had his previous schooling in Russia. He was scornful of his training there and went out of his way to tell me how much he valued and appreciated what he was picking up from me in an American institution. Another was an earnest, struggling, unqualified, obviously poor, black to whom I charitably awarded a grade of D. He disappeared from class attendance, but I looked him up through his mother, helped him a bit with a little money, and persuaded him to continue his education. However, another student—older, glib, well dressed, a teacher himself, attempting to get credits for his profession—would vanish at the halfway point of every session. I had to call him on this, and at the next examination he and the student sitting next to him gave such preposterous, out-of-the-blue, false, identical answers that I knew one had copied the other. He quit on me in a huff, loudly accusing me of racial prejudice.

In addition to the San Diego State, teaching Chinese history

158

venture, I had to turn to athletics to keep me busy. I would joke that I played golf and tennis to keep myself out of the bars. Bonita, near Chula Vista, had a convenient golf course, and one of the U.S. Navy links in San Diego had been named after my old NROTC commander in the unit at Yale. I believe that San Diego County boasted at having more golf courses than any other comparable area in the country.

North Island Naval Air Station was great for an extended, noon-hour tennis date. I got routinely beaten by Comdr. Robert Hutchins, the legal officer for the air station. He and I were old acquaintances from Tsingtao, China, where I had been the ComNavWesPac admiral's aide and he had been the legal officer. Now in Coronado we were both pursuing academic and intellectual objectives. He as a legal officer was intent on passing the examination for the California bar, anticipating his retirement. I was not ready to call it quits in the Marine Corps, but knew that someday there would be another career for me. I had completed all the course work possible, so I was preparing at the Coronado city library for my American University, Ph.D., comprehensive examinations to be conducted in absentia.

*　　*　　*

In the naval and military services in these years there were many schools, courses, and other instructional opportunities that one could attend, or work to avoid, either within his own organization or by filling a slot in the quota for that schooling. I saw how this was operating and took advantage of my chance at attendance. I volunteered for a month's course back at Quantico, primarily for summer training of reserve officers, but with applicability to the amphibious mission of LFTU. Quantico and Washington, D.C., were worthwhile, familiar grounds for me.

Another venture was to fill a quota at the U.S. Army gas warfare sub-unit of Camp Detrick, Maryland, in the desert at Tooele,

159

Utah. I have a feeling that we were occupying and utilizing the shabby site of the WW II camp for unjustly-imprisoned Japanese-Americans. Too, I sense that today the concept of gas warfare has been cooled down, but concede that somewhere, somehow, a capability in offensive or defensive warfare must be sustained. Neither do I hear much now about flame throwers in infantry or tank warfare. They surely had been important in WW II. I was acquainted with the commanding officer here at Tooele, and we had a surprise meeting as Pentagon veterans. The climax of the course was the conduct of an artillery shoot, only one piece. Tethered on a distant peak were three sheep. We students were mustered to watch. Sure enough, the gas killed them. A more worthwhile episode in this time was a bus ride into Salt Lake City. I enjoyed my first and only look at the Mormon Temple, had a glimpse of the Great Salt Lake, and remembered my history of the nearby junction of the first railroad across the country.

*　　*　　*

In the spring of 1965 the annual amphibious exercise, termed "Silver Lance," was held at Camp Pendleton. LFTU participated by providing referees and observers. I was put in charge of the guest bureau, inviting the approved VIP attendees, escorting them before and at the assault upon the beach, publicizing the event, and persuading politicians and newsmen of the readiness and preeminence of the Marine Corps in a new vision of warfare.

I had earlier attended a guidance session for the exercise at Fleet Marine Force Pacific, in Oahu, so I knew what was coming. General Krulak had told me to take back the word that this was to be a new type of exercise. It was not to be a simple amphibious assault. The emphasis in all our armed forces was upon counterinsurgency. The president himself had decreed this revolutionary change. Even Cooks and Bakers School was ordered to include a counterinsurgency course. And at this Camp Pendleton exercise

160

the commanders and troops—besides chasing the enemy, seizing the high ground and holding it, and continuing the attack to a new objective—were to be confronted with such problems as, "We protest the destruction of our hospital," "What are you going to do about restoring water and power?" and "We are not your enemy but an oppressed minority and need your help."

California Congressman and Marine major reservist, Pete McCloskey, played the part of mayor or governor of the invaded nation. I admired him then and again, when he was to duel with Pat Robertson, the rabid fundamentalist. Best exposition of this approach, what became the Marine Corps emphasis in Vietnam, was "Winning The Hearts And Minds Of The People." Antiwar protesters were to scoff at this, but good soldiers, sailors, and Marines were to try very hard at it.

A few days before the landing exercise a brigade at sea was diverted, interrupting its participation in the exercise. I recall that this was incident to the buildup of combat infantry for Vietnam, not just commitment to the MAAG mission or early helicopter support. It looked like another era had begun, and I determined what this might mean for me. On the books, in the theoretical requirements for the artillery regimental commander, it was specified that he be nuclear-qualified. That meant that I had to get into a special, Fort Sill, Oklahoma, U.S. Army course. This seemed very bureaucratic, but Marines had eight-inch howitzers and there was a dreamy belief in—maybe—tactical nuclear warfare. So I attended the course at Fort Sill, which was new, interesting, and professional for me; and got the secondary, nuke-qualified, Military Occupational Specialty. It never did me much good, and by that don't get me wrong—I'm not regretting that nukes were not to be employed. At least now I was qualified, but in Vietnam the requirement certainly was ignored.

There was, however, a real route to move on from Coronado and get to Vietnam. A sailor might say he rattled his chains, but a Marine would work his bolt. I got in touch with Col. Fred Karch, a first leader of the Vietnam intervention, whom I had served under at Camp Lejeune. Just to make sure of things I also wrote General Krulak, now the FMF commander in the Pacific, that I was not needed in LFTU and requested Vietnam. The word got back to personnel assignment in Washington, and it looked like I was soon to be reassigned. But there was a delay—a replacement had first to come aboard. It was exasperating to have to wait, but when my orders actually arrived, I was so elated that I unthinkingly dove into the shallow end of the swimming pool at the Hotel Del Coronado and gave my nose a bit of a battering. So now, not as aide to the chairman of the Joint Chiefs of Staff, but on a routine assignment, I was to get to the Third Marine Division at Danang.

*　　*　　*

Before any telling of my Vietnam experience, I turn to Barbara Tuchman, great authoress, superb historian. She writes of a major problem for historian and journalists—that the negatives, mistakes, stupidities, misjudgments often overwhelm the positive and even the heroic. The daily newspapers seek readership, based on reporting on the big scale, of crime, accidents, threats, crises. Tabloids thrive on the scandal, failures or defeats that befall individuals. So, then, with my Vietnam, of course only recalled and recorded at my own, personal, limited, 1965–66 level.

I endeavor to remember my time in Danang over a great variety of experiences. What were my duties meant to be? I first muse about a world of the entertaining, unimportant, futile, and useless. Then I must look at the shameful, the sorrowful, and misguided aspects of our Vietnam venture. Here indeed are the negatives and the mistakes. But the historian or reporter must understand the context of time and place and not just scoff or scorn. Finally, however, I truly strive to highlight the heroic, the worthwhile, and the honorable.

Certainly we tried. The antiwar protestors who came late and

162

from outside, in their criticisms of our leaders, our soldiers, and our very motives in Vietnam—can take a back seat for now. I assert that the mistakes of today are usually just continuations of errors that were made in the past. Go back to Sen. Joe McCarthy if you seek a real devil in American political life. Anything was acceptable in his passionate pursuit of anti-communism. The worst of dictators and regimes were just fine as long as they fit the anti-communist mold. Now, as well, consider another stunt of leadership: "Tell me what I want to hear." Of course resort can always be made to Deniability if something reaches me that I do not want to hear. So join me as I arrived in Danang in the fall of 1965.

*　　*　　*

The billet for me was called Base Defense Coordinator. Again I found myself in a non-Table of Organization spot. I was on the staff of III MAF, an amphibious force, still in the process of building up from the two-battalion expeditionary brigade that had come ashore in April. It would grow to include many more of the units of the Third Marine Division and the First Marine Aircraft Wing. We Marines were still getting organized and receiving the reinforcements which staged through Okinawa. Senior officers were billeted in a corridor length of rooms that resembled a motel, and for a spell it was necessary to double up, alternating the use of bunks and rooms.

Well, base defense? One might say this actually just meant security, and security could mean a little bit of everything. There seemed two primary responsibilities for me. Number one was paperwork. Every night a dispatch was required to higher echelons on our day and night patrolling in the territory surrounding Danang, giving encouragement to the populace, boosting morale, showing our supporting presence. Every company had to specify how many men, for how many man-hours, patrolled in specific areas of the countryside. This was "Pacification." It was also called

163

trying to "win the hearts and minds of the people." I do not know who first used this phrase, but Marines were diligent about living up to it.

A physical aspect of our base defense, that is to say, our security, involved surveying and construction of a chain-link fence around the Danang airfield, home of our headquarters until most could displace to a new, large, bunker a few miles inland. Before my arrival a sizable Viet Cong force had broken through the old perimeter fence and destroyed several USAF planes and equipment. This area had been the defense responsibility of the South Vietnamese, but by my time this vulnerability called for a battalion-size security force. A contract had been signed with an engineering firm, also involved in other Vietnam airfield construction, to complete this job. Here in the Danang area the firm was supervised by a retired U.S. Army brigadier general, in civilian status. He had been the army's beach-master at landings in Okinawa, so Marines had reason to be familiar and helpful with his project.

The actual survey was conducted by a Filipino work crew, and it seemed my duty to oversee them. A nice, curving, security fence about the airfield perimeter would have best filled our needs. The trouble was that the surrounding rice paddies were usually straight-lined and divided by firm, raised little barriers or paths. The farmers did not like to see their fields split apart or appropriated arbitrarily, and the survey crew and fence constructors did not think much of jagged corners and change of directions for the fence. Details vanish in memory, but there had to be negotiation, argument, delay, and necessary compensation to be figured and awarded. This involved a new staff responsibility: "Civil Affairs."

Soon other demands were laid on Civil Affairs. The existent trails and roads around Danang were so inadequate that resort had to be made to rock acquisition, rock crushing in a big, complex rig and tedious spreading and build-up over the necessary miles. Our trucks and tanks were too heavy for the existent road pattern. I suppose the rock was locally available, but we had trouble with the rock-crushing task. The rig and quarry were owned by a Vietnam-ese lady, an absentee, who endeavored to get her money's worth and more for the work. Tanks had a difficult time in this I Corps area. Venture off the unstable, narrow little roads into rice paddy land, even the dry or unused fields, and just watch the tanks sink down and away. Another hazard, and since it affected movement and transport and thus security, was that fine sand, which ruined brake bands of our vehicles. We were very handicapped in jeep and truck maintenance and availability.

Another group of tenants at the field were USAF facilities, planes, and personnel. All well and good that a fence bar off in-truders along the distant perimeter, but the air force did not think much about a new fence in front of their hangars or one which chopped up access from the buildings and storage areas behind them. That pre-existent, partial fence around the field continued inadequate to prevent guerrillas from breaking in to destroy air-craft. So a full battalion had to be assigned around-the-clock guard duties. Later the battalion had split duties, leaving only two com-panies on the field. When there was no further attack, how was the general to decide that they could be relieved and sent on more pressing duties?

And so it was throughout Danang, Chu Lai, and Phu Bai, the three enclaves of the Third Marine Division. There were HAWK anti-aircraft batteries on peaks (never needed in my time, how-ever) and there were bridges to be guarded from sabotage. Some-one had to figure out how best to utilize war dogs, patiently awaiting a worthwhile mission. The safety of Red Cross girls in their billets had to be ensured. Hotels for visiting VIPs were orga-nized, but I successfully protested that I should not also be as-signed the extra duty of hotel manager for this purpose.

There was the threat of land mines that became increasingly dangerous. The trick on the enemy's part was to let a jeep pass by outward bound to the front, but then to emplace the mine to catch it on the return trip at the end of a day.

Protection of the major ammunition supplies had to be built up and enlarged, a big concern. Would a fence be enough or did there also have to be nighttime sentries in holes? And did protection mean consolidating the dumps of shells and bombs—remember aircraft at Pearl Harbor and General MacArthur's fleet at Clark Field devastatingly caught by the Japs because they were bunched together for better defense against an internal attack? Or was it best to disperse ammo far and wide in extravagant bunkers to minimize destruction in a blow up?

Thinking of bunkers, an elaborate one was constructed laboriously for the headquarters of the division as it displaced inland away from the beach. Subordinate elements all were ordered to build bunkers of heavy logs and sandbagged reinforcing roofs. These seemed more like shelters against artillery or air attack, but one cannot fault their necessity. They were used as safe living quarters for exhausted Marines who might have to board helicopters for a daytime raid; work on their bunkers, foxholes, and barbed wire defenses on return: and go on patrol at night.

This inevitably brings to mind a startling inequity. There were also other Marines present, uniformed in wash khaki, not fatigues and steel helmets, and living downtown quite comfortably. They probably had been assigned from the Military Assistance Advisory Group or the embassy in Saigon, on the mission of security for a few MAAG officers. They not only were on special per diem allowances, but also were given air transportation back and forth to the commissary and post exchange in Saigon, since they had no mess facilities of their own. Hard to take for Third Marine Division troops, for whom the general did not allow any liberty whatsoever in the city. In those days Marines were disciplined, brave, and long-suffering. In my time there were never any incidents of "fragging," as were later reported.

A great hazard was the positioning of field artillery pieces, a special interest and concern for me. They were necessarily separated from each other in the disposition of a battery. The enemy intruder could be a stark-naked, Viet Cong soldier, on a suicide mission, at night, with an explosive device, sneaking in on a single, chosen, howitzer pit among the many howitzers of the regiment. The same with water points, gas depots, and bridges.

With regard to incoming fire, occasionally we would receive a round, probably mortar fire and never doing much damage. An artilleryman's responsibility was to promptly investigate the angle of entry and backplot the direction from which the round was fired—and fire back or send out a patrol. Well, this Base Defense Coordinator, without a jeep, with scores of miles of front, being outside of the artillery regiment, could never do a thing about such an event—only talk about it at the daily command briefing.

Acquisition of targets was the artillery objective. We had only a scarce number of observation aircraft. At night, imagined targets were picked out for H & I fires (Harassing and Interdiction). I fear that these never did much good. And the gunners had a restriction placed upon them—that they hold up for clearance from the Vietnamese I Corps command in case the target or area might be friendlies.

I move along in my musing. A new naval hospital was being established on the beach. Of course, it had to be well protected along with an adjoining, pathetic Vietnamese orphanage facility that only a few of us even knew about. Neither did we seem able to deal with the problem of hordes of peasants crowding into enclosures filled with shabby tents or cardboard shelters. One such frightfully unsanitary encampment had only a single water spigot for hundreds of refugees. I once had to deflect or answer a curious newsman on what we should or could have done about this problem. It was about the time of another, well-publicized statement by a Marine: "We had to burn down the village to save it."

Of greater prominence on the beach was the site of the new corps headquarters, only just started up during my tour. It is difficult now to remember or describe the physical scene, but the beach was also the spot for Sunday afternoon liberty, meaning swimming parties. It was usually too difficult a trip for the deserving infantry to get to, so maybe most of the beer went to rear echelon guys. Down the beach was Monkey Mountain, a few miles distant from us and probably a good hiding place for the enemy. In relative security on the beach, close in to the city of Danang itself, were our helicopters. One evening from across a sort of lagoon, in a hut of the public information officer and in the company of several journalists, we were forced to watch from armchairs the embarrassing fireworks display at Marble Mountain, as many of the wing's helicopters were blown up.

Of the city of Danang itself, there is a plentitude to report; but please continue to accept these episodes or observations as simply my reporting on security.

Returning to that matter of surveying for the new security fence, it was found necessary to move a civilian cemetery that was in the way. It was a frightful mess, not a cemetery, but just a mass of fresh graves on a muddy hilltop, with little pieces of prayer paper placed on each, as is the oriental practice. It was also an only place where that horde of pathetic refugees could squat to take a—O.K., *defecate.* On one rainy Sunday morning I joined the solitary, forlorn, ragged gravedigger, (or re-digger), with his handcart and shovel. It was an all-time tragic, lamentable scene. I could not help him. It seemed an endless job. What was he to do with the remains of remains? He had only a couple of stacks of cheap, cardboard shoeboxes for his loads. The rain had made a mess of the boxes.

There were other solutions for security. The French were still a presence in Danang, needed for running the power generation plant and importing Esso gasoline for the considerable population of the city. They enjoyed their athletic and dining club, Le Cercle Sportif, and had a small resort on a nearby lake reportedly with wine, cabanas, water-skiing, and girls in bikinis. One evening I was invited downtown to join them, donning a civilian suit which I had brought along since such was acceptable attire on my earlier trips to Saigon with Gen. Maxwell Taylor. We were entertained in a French home, during which the power failed. Never mind, they knew how to fix matters. The solution was in an agreement. They knew how to get along with the other side.

Also present were members of the United Nations truce supervisory team of Danang—an Indian, a Canadian, and a Pole. The team, like counterpart teams in Saigon, Hanoi, and some place across the demilitarized zone from us, was supposed to count and report numbers of trucks, pieces of ordnance, rifles, people, and buggy whips—everything—that was being imported by either side in violation of the Geneva truce agreement. It was a useless task. To pass the time their favorite activity seemed to be spirited volleyball games. The ironic, final, little twist on things was that the Canadian, who had been a Quantico, senior amphibious course, fellow student of ours, was surly, impatient, non-communicating; but the Communist Pole was jovial, fun, a good guy.

We had a couple of tasks that were basically related to security and which I cannot overlook. A business offering, through the Pentagon, required that we test an array of buried microphones—sonic detectors—to see if they were worthwhile in detecting an enemy moving about on foot beyond our lines at night. It was a tedious nuisance to haul troops back for this. Of course, there was everything one could imagine moving about at night beyond our lines. Peasants, children, water buffalo, pigs, chickens, moving carts. But how to identify friend from foe? I have stumbled into that most essential and difficult problem of all, identifying the enemy. They all might look the same. The Viet Cong tactic was to hide among the populace. A patrol entering a village on a "winning the hearts and minds of the people" mission might well encounter two brothers. One would appear welcoming, cooperatively offer an opinion on where he thought the enemy might be. He might greet the patrol with a smile and cool water. The other would be retiring, uncooperative, impatient, wishing we would go away. As often as not, brother A was the red-hot, wanting to kill us; brother B would be an innocent giving the wrong impression or afraid to show his loyalty.

Exasperation or indifference would sometimes overcome our troops. On patrol some bored and uncaring trooper might choose to run his pocket radio at loud blast, scornfully or ignorantly advertising his presence. Impatiently some might kill the wrong villager, or would rule all to be in the same boat, so "get in the truck, we're taking you in!" I visited South Vietnamese counterparts a few times at their headquarters, where those villagers were "taken in." Usually no one was about. At the time of Tet, in February 1966, our allies actually turned against us, threatening a real revolt. The attitude of this, I Corps, South Vietnamese, counterpart command gave me the impression that any peasants brought in by Yanks were probably enemy, so why bother further. It was easier to judge arbitrarily or without further investigation. It was rumored that "they" would sometimes simply put a victim into a handy helicopter and shove him out into the Gulf of Tonkin.

Security or base defense somehow included some strange manifestations. I attended a high school graduation when the general was overwhelmed with other matters. I had traveled to Danang from the U.S. on air transport with a fellow passenger, a famed, female, war correspondent. Dickie Chappel was sadly killed on patrol, while asserting her equality and sharing the lot of men in combat. When it was heard that I knew her, I ran a memorial service with a full group of war correspondents in attendance. Martha Raye, the cheerful, supportive entertainer, arrived one evening by helicopter in the worst of rain squalls. Yes, I met her.

Other Hollywood stars visited to cheer the troops, and we once had a large contingent for a major show that came to entertain. They certainly cheered the troops, but our general and plenty of others were irritated, when after assembling a large audience from all over the division, the producer informed the audience, "That was an unsatisfactory rehearsal for our TV recording. The troops should stay for a repeat!" Politicians visited; some invited by our own Defense Department to be persuaded as to the purpose and success of our very presence in Vietnam. I once had to escort an unpleasant movie star, but I also had the pleasure of meeting and establishing a friendship with a great one, Charlton Heston. And I had a personal helo reconn with thoughtful, sympathetic Sen. Jacob Javits of New York.

A Washington or Saigon delegation once called, and we were surprised by their insistence on a rare security precaution. For their own travel for just a few miles between beach and the Third Marine Division headquarters bunker, they adjudged the short jeep trip was not acceptable. They required a helicopter ride, and not one, but two, in case one should be brought down. It reminded me of a Defense Department decree that if one had had a stateside Top Secret clearance, he could not be assigned to Vietnam for two years. (Not much attention was ever paid to that.) It was hard anyway to discover any USMC field officers who did not have Top Secret clearance in the first place.

*   *   *

At the halfway point in my tour I was shifted from Base Defense Coordinator to becoming the intelligence officer, the G-2, of the division. In many ways my duties or preoccupations did not change. I gave daily intelligence briefings at the staff meetings, and it was important to get up early enough so that I knew all the overnight developments that the general did. Inevitably my initiative or awareness did not have much to do with intelligence on the enemy, but put me on the spot for comment on operational, G-3 events. I attempted analysis on a map as to where enemy groups might assemble, and their possible routes for infiltration. This earned me credit perhaps for initiative, but did not deserve anything for what was purely conjecture. Another resort was to go to downtown Danang to buy the Hong Kong newspaper. No great secrets to uncover, but it quickly and more accurately reflected the Hanoi and Viet Cong world than anything we were getting out of Saigon, Pearl Harbor, or Washington.

The extent of the division front was so great that there were inevitable gaps. I wished later that I had followed up on an instinct to take off my colonel's eagles and absent myself for a few days to circle the entire perimeter on foot, where the privates were, to know more about those gaps. General Walt, our respected, experienced, veteran, dedicated, tireless leader, had an advantage. At dawn after some ambush, flurry, or threat on the front, he would arrive on the scene by his helicopter for his own appraisal or disciplining. The regimental, battalion, and maybe even the company commanders were simply bypassed.

I summon up Barbara Tuchman again. She warned of preoccupation with the negatives, criticisms, futilities, and problems in combat reporting, but explained or made allowance that individuals, historians, journalists, and memoir writers will have vastly different attitudes, interpretations, inclusions, and omissions in their accounts. I realize how different my own, brief and shallow Vietnam story varies from those of other writers, the monographs, and official, detailed, Marine Corps Historical Division accounts. And so, I explain. "My" Vietnam was the climax to my military career and so I continue with my own stories—some invidious, some funny, and some heroic. My security stories will seem to go on and on. I get a bit windy.

Khe Sanh years later became the scene of most contested, heroic defense by Marines. In 1965–66 I felt it was a probable site for undercover, secret, meetings by jeep journey over number so-and-so route of the national system—between leaders among our Saigon, South Vietnamese allies, and the other side. Weather was too bad for our helo to set down, but we then first identified Khe Sanh as an important spot. It was located generally just south of the inland end of the demilitarized zone. That national route seemed a good trail to test, to reconnoiter. Despite a suggestion that such an operation required a full battalion with artillery support, a special, heroic friend, Lt. Colonel Ding-Dong Bell, led it out as a walk in the sun. The Viet Cong were, instead, infiltrating by us, inland, down the Ho Chi Minh Trail all the way to the Saigon and the southern delta areas. Of course, in latter years the road to Khe Sanh was a deadly one, but in this time the greatest hazard for the battalion at the finish were urchins pushing soda pop upon the thirsty troops—containing broken glass chips.

Somewhat akin to my trip to Khe Sanh was a visit to an outpost, inland, in the impassible jungle, maybe intended to overlook that Ho Chi Minh Trail. It was on a small, bare peak, absolutely isolated, practically unreachable on foot. The current enterprise was to helicopter in a 105-mm howitzer. The personnel here were South Vietnamese, probably afraid for their lives, under the guidance of a showy, unmilitary-appearing German, an ex-French foreign legionnaire? CIA? There appeared to be no aggressive patrolling, and it certainly was no position for a howitzer.

I tell another story, certainly originating with the participants, passed into other ears and through other mouths, retold to me, occurring well after my time in country, maybe embellished, but essentially true. An outstanding major, completing his half-tour as an infantry battalion executive officer, was summoned to Saigon for a strange assignment. With only a couple of U.S. troopers, guards and communicators, but a motley assembly of South Vietnamese (including as the essential heart and purpose of the mission, several whores) he was to lead the group into Cambodia. The point was to entice certain targeted personnel with the whores and then assassinate them. Nothing came of this enterprise. At Phnom Penh he sought help and a return lift to Saigon from an old acquaintance, the gunnery sergeant of the U.S. Embassy guard. After a consult inside with the charge d'affaires, the sergeant returned with a long face. "Sorry, Major, no help."

He queried why not. "Because there are no Americans in Cambodia." Next, the major was referred to Air America (a.k.a.

Air Asia) as a commercial airline for a lift home for all. How to pay for it? Here is a Bank of America credit card, unfortunately expired. Anyway it was accepted as supposed payment for regular airline travel. All returned to Saigon. Hospitalized after his return, he was rebuked in disbelief by General Abrams for this story. The general might have been the top commander in country, but he was out of the loop.

Phu Bai was a smaller enclave close to Hue, the historic capital of the nation and its culture. The command here took special lead in pacification, commendably and energetically training and sponsoring joint patrols of Marines and Viet soldiers. In that time I sponsored my own group of fellow officers in an adventure we called "poor man's R and R." I am light-hearted here, but I want to credit in Hue the efforts of the doctors, physicians, of Project Hope, doing their best to win hearts and minds and cure bodies.

On another trip to Hue our group was invited to a South Vietnamese command for a grand Sunday celebratory luncheon in a palace on the Perfume River. It was a nasty shock to be invited, after the sumptuous meal, to view the battlefield nearby. One wondered how many of those bloody bodies were innocent peasants and how many were guerrilla infiltrators. And certainly later, Hue became the site of bloody combat with brave effort by the best of Marines—but that was after my time.

I also include, with regard to the problem of security and identifying the enemy, a tale with a lighter note. A dedicated, competent and energetic, battalion commander. Lt. Col. Woody Woodruff, had been chasing a couple of suspects that he thought he had cornered for questioning. His description to General Walt of the scene was unforgettable. "There they were, General, sweatin' like whores in church!"

Danang saw some petty little events about which we could not be proud, but which in the interest of full disclosure, I must recount. In the very headquarters of III MAF some imagined that there was enemy tunneling going on underground. I was directed to get engineers busy with sonic detection equipment. They indeed "told them what they wanted to hear," and the investigation began to get out of hand. A backhoe was called in, and the heart of the parade was made into a mess. General Walt had been away, and when he returned, he was not happy.

Units were often dispatched into the countryside, on missions now more purposeful than just guarding the airfield. On one occasion a command post was shifted repeatedly, too many times in one day. That commander was concerned too much about security—his own personal security. We were a mixed bag of ground and aviation, and sometimes there were questions about who should decide the commitment of helicopters, or why were there not more aerial observation craft for the artillery. But we all had a laugh once when an observer excitedly reported sighting of an enemy tank. It turned out to be a water buffalo.

Villagers near Danang revered a Buddhist shrine, sort of a gazebo, which was passed and observed daily by patrolling Marines. Shots were taken at them, a few days would pass, and then more rounds would threaten again. The frustrated troops eventually retaliated with some damage to the shrine, including the image of Buddha. So a delegation of elders arrived to complain bitterly to the general, resulting in an order that a squad be assigned day and night as security guard for the image and the structure. In time, with no further threats, the squad was relieved. But, oh oh, the last to depart spoiled all, set pacification back a hundred years, by defecating on Buddha's lap. Again the elders, with even more indignant protests. A replacement Buddha was procured in Japan—it was bizarre, vividly multicolored, chubby, and cheap. Presentation day was marred by the concurrent arrival of some Washington VIPs. Anyway, the new Buddha looked like Porky the Pig. You know, "Th', Th', That's All, Folks!"

I do not overlook Chu Lai. We had a command arrangement there that would have been rejected—rather, *condemned,* at any staff school. Ground and aviation units were present. They were normally cooperative. After a 1966, enemy, night attack on the perimeter, all elements manned foxholes and guarded the wire. My old friend Fred Karch could order his infantry to obey his security decisions. But the wing units were not under his command, and in time chose to do things their way. If another, real assault had ever taken place, there might have been disaster. Fred Karch also stated to me that he had never received a basic order or directive laying out Chu Lai's command status and responsibilities. He held only an outmoded, G-4 directive on logistics arrangements.

I got away from Danang with a rather special departure. This colonel was treated a bit too royally at Danang airfield, around which I had been mundanely supervising that Filipino survey crew for the new security fence. It was now being operated like a terminal, the enlisted Marines being overly attentive with me. They made me wait for my flight in a regular VIP waiting room. Trouble was, no one was alert for the actual departure, and so I had to be sped along in a special jeep, making the air force lift, already warming up his engines, the doors and ladder closed. It was a relief to bid Vietnam farewell as I was hoisted up through a trap door, ending up in the very cockpit with the pilots. We transited Okinawa, my long-ago exit point from mainland China, but about which I had little familiarity despite my several years in the Far East. Last leg: Hawaii to San Diego.

*   *   *

After the usual nine months in Vietnam, I returned to Coronado for the second time around, or rather the fourth. I had been given orders to Washington again, to the Chief of Naval Operations for an office for long-range naval planning. Long-range naval planning did not sit well with me one bit, so I investigated and found that the incumbent colonel in a billet at Naval Amphibious Forces Pacific was sick, due for transfer, or declaring for retirement. So it was with a feeling of relief that I could resume at

176

Coronado, not having to sell and move a home again, and thus satisfy my wife.

I was designated the Marine Officer at ComPhibPac. In the same office space I was joined with two USMC comrades. One oversaw combat loading planning for the amphibs in the Pacific and perhaps actual embarkation for the buildup proceeding now in I Corps, Vietnam. The other's duties are not remembered, but could not have been onerous. He was an aviator who took me for my first and only ride in a jet fighter—with all the necessary indoctrination, use of oxygen, and bailout procedure. I acquired a new and special respect for aviators.

Marine Corps reinforcements for Vietnam were proceeding routinely, and there was more serious combat building up since the time I had been in Danang. An army brigade in Hawaii was to be another unit sent on, so for their final rehearsal and training I was sent to Hawaii to observe the brigade's readiness. Attendance was really in response to a courtesy invitation to the admiral, but he declined and sent me.

There first occurred an interlude for me on Oahu during which I accidentally ran into my old boss, Gen. Maxwell Taylor, conferring with the presidential advisor Clark Clifford as I was passing through. I have to believe that this might have been an early meeting on how to get out of the Vietnam involvement—but this took many more years and lives.

The army exercise was on relatively undeveloped and unspoiled Molokai. In a surprise reunion for me I ran into a group of college classmates residing or visiting there on the island. Too, it was surprising and interesting to watch some Japanese-Americans holding a traditional celebration ceremony in the moonlight on a grassy field with only the several churches in the background. Present also were a group of youngsters awaiting arrival of a number of yachts finishing a California to Hawaii race. The youngsters, the yachts, the Japanese ceremony, and my classmates hardly had a thing to do with the army brigade's exercise. When I returned to Coronado, it did not seem to make much difference anyway.

The U.S. Navy endeavored to give its very best support to the troops on the ground in Vietnam. The buildup of a riverine force for the delta region involved amphibious craft especially modified to detect and chase the enemy. A special command vessel for shallow waters had been developed, but also memorable was the planning for high-speed, jet-fan, air-cushioned hovercraft. I took some trial runs in one in San Diego Bay. It worked—could pass over water and perhaps also transit low, level, sandy soil. Only troubles were that the fan threw up such a shower of spray that the best of windshield wipers was inadequate and that it made a racket that would awaken the dead. Any guerrillas in the Vietnam delta would be alerted far ahead to its approach.

Naval gunfire support was a tool that had been perfected in WW II. A team was sent from Washington to study, investigate, and possibly help in this type of warfare. I accompanied this team to a naval weapons base in Corona, California, for a seminar or planning conference on the possibilities for naval gunfire. And is it remembered that battleships (maybe only one, but that was enough) were called out of mothballs to render naval gunfire support for the campaigning in Vietnam. It is pretty hard to try and kill guerrillas from a battleship platform, even if you could identify who and where they might be. A research think-tank in San Diego obtained a contract to aggrandize the potential of naval gunfire, to help save the day in Vietnam. Recalling today what I had experienced and instinctively knew about ground combat in the jungles of Asia, I feel ashamed that I accepted some compensation, pay from this commercial outfit. My own evaluation of the battle for Vietnam goes like this: It is like putting a battleship in Santa Monica Bay with the mission of killing all the left-handed persons in Pasadena—mind you, only the *left*-handed ones.

*　　*　　*

Thinking of my past and realizing that I had better get on with a plan for retirement, I sought an education in computer programming. I had built on my education in history, worked on it at night school at The American University in Washington, even passed the Ph.D. comprehensives, and had a fling at teaching about the foreigners of the 19th century in Formosa. However, the teaching experiment at San Diego State did not quite satisfy.

A fellow Marine told me of a course in computer programming in downtown San Diego, that I could commute to by that neat ferry ride. I wanted to keep up with the generation of the young, and the idea that it was an adventure and challenge in mathematics intrigued me. I did not excel in the course, grasping the big picture but stumbling a bit with some basic mistakes. In case you do not know it, or to dramatize my new acquisition of knowledge—I discovered that a computer works with the speed of light and the search goes through gates, yes or no, the light on or off, the glass empty or full. There are only two options. I guess I was back to the binary system. However, at this time in Coronado I had no idea what I would do with this skill.

As Marine Officer on the ComPhibPac staff a particular task was picked out for me that was responsible, interesting, and temporarily preoccupying. I was appointed as the senior member of a general court-martial board. Two cases remain worthwhile reporting. About both of them I apologize for a critical attitude which might make me seem a wise guy, a smart-aleck appearing to know better than my superiors. First of all, the revised Uniform Court of Military Justice regulations minimized the participation, brainpower, intelligence, and action of the senior member. The members of general courts-martial were to say nothing, make no comment, think not—just vote, and obey the prosecutor, known as the judge advocate.

I knew the judge advocate in this case and we respected each other. However, he too strictly instructed us to be on time in assembling after a noon break. Then he himself was late, after an apparent martini luncheon. Not a good start to proceedings. A naval corpsman had been brought before us on a strange charge. Allegedly he had been accused of being disrespectful in his performance in the obstetrical ward during births at the naval hospital. He had joked or told dirty stories, and several mothers had gotten together to protest his behavior. I felt that many doctors, maybe to ease the tension, or divert from the sensitivity of the moment, sometimes will joke or make inappropriate comment. So I voted not guilty, and also was not a dumb, silent, senior member of the court. I admit that I influenced my juniors, naval officers, most of whom I knew well, that this accused should go free.

The other court had a similar result. The finding and my comment at trial end seemed reasons why I got relieved as the senior member of the court. It was about the last act or action in my Marine Corps career. This time the accused was black, a first class petty officer, with many years service, accompanied in the courtroom by an obviously supportive, clean-cut, attractive wife and children. He had been on liberty in Los Angeles, admittedly in a hotel, at a rendezvous, or assignation, for a fee, with someone he should not have been with. The someone turned out to an hermaphrodite who had entrapped him, and the hermaphrodite's associate had broken into the room threatening the good sailor. He cleaned house with them. The shore patrol picked him up. It was hard to believe that a fair and complete, formal, pretrial investigation had been conducted prior to his appearance before us. He had been set up and committed a mistake, but he and his family did not deserve such an endangerment to his career and future. Again I coached the junior members, although it was hardly necessary, into how they should vote. Before the not guilty verdict, I gave the accused and his worried family a big reassuring smile.

TWELVE

Retirement, Oxford, Travel, and The Marine Military Academy

When last heard of, there I was, out of Vietnam and returned to San Diego. But wait a minute, go back. We have been through all this Coronado, San Diego, recitation of events before. Recall that my final, remembered episodes at PhibPac were those two general courts-martial. It was time to take a new look at things. What about the future? Now I was about to escape again, this time into retirement. There certainly had to be some sort of a ceremony associated with retirement, after those years of service and about which to be proud. So it was for me. I had never had much reason to visit or to be involved in the business of the San Diego Recruit Depot, but indeed along with Camp Pendleton it was the primary focus of the Marines in Southern California. The commanding general was absent on that last day of June, 1968, when my great adventure in the Corps was finished.

The chief of staff, however, was Col. Roy Thompson, who invited me to be the reviewing officer for the full parade of graduating recruits, of those in mid-training, and of newest recruits. The band was magnificent and transported me back to glorious assemblies at 8th and I Streets, Washington, D.C.; to the parade ground at Quantico; and to ceremonies in the Second Marine Division, Camp Lejeune, North Carolina. There was much that tugged at my heart that day. Those about to graduate were well disciplined and sharp in their new uniforms, their bearing, and their appearance.

For many parents attending graduation it is literally true that, after the creation of new personalities and perfected physiques, mothers and fathers are unable to recognize their own sons. At the other end of the scale and of that big, long, impressive parade were boots in their first weeks of training, in utilities, just beginning to learn what it was all about.

I had initially known Roy Thompson in 1947 in our billet within the former British Legation compound in Peking. We were then in the 2nd Battalion, Fifth Marines, and wore the special 5th Marines aiguillette, awarded that unit in WW I France. It was meaningful to have Col. Thompson as a presentee along with both Col. Hope Kirk—call him my father in WW II—and Captain Eddie Pearce, USN, who had brought me up in Tsingtao, China. These were the most colorful of characters. Hope had made the Marines "fun" for us, if you can believe it. He had shown us how to take care of our men, in war and in peace. Eddie, under full sail would declaim that, anyway, he would have preferred being a bishop rather than an admiral. He was a talented Japanese linguist and had performed importantly in naval intelligence.

The parade was led by the Recruit Depot band, and there was such a number of recruits that I trooped the line, not on foot, but with Roy in a jeep, standing up. I get emotional about this now, for truly I was the reviewing officer at a ceremony surpassing those occasions at HQMC, Quantico, and Camp Lejeune. And be it noted that even after our many years and campaigns in the Pacific, after Korea, and ultimately after Vietnam—Marines never were accorded victory, homecoming parades. No Broadway nor Market Street celebrations for the U.S. Marine Corps. Heck, I had hardly ever donned my marmeluke sword and was ignorant of the manual of the sword.

*   *   *

In this account, which I offer as an autobiography, although I have wanted it to have, as well, the nature of a naval and military memoir—I cannot stop right now. The Marine Corps service was over, but I have more to recite. There is much that is important personally for me myself to be set down. I am the sort that looks forward to what comes next, and I can and often forget what I have done. So I endeavor now to dramatize the historical and geographical in my new adventures and wanderings. Let that uniform and its accompanying sword be memories. But there surely were places to go and things for me to do.

It is time for me to set a few priorities. First things first. Oh, all right, the Second Time Around is what matters, and our meeting, courtship, wedding, and future together goes gloriously on and on. Else and I had met at a Lucky Lager tennis tournament at La Costa, the Southern California resort for golf, tennis, a spa, and luxurious accommodations. Pancho Segura, the classic and classy tennis professional, had shifted his base there from the Beverly Hills Tennis Club. Else's group was invited there by Pancho, while I with my pals came from the informal association we had for the game on the courts of Coronado's Hotel Del. After tennis I was confronted by an assembly of several La Costans irate about the war in Vietnam and wanting to engage me in a debate thereon. They forcefully disagreed with anyone who might have participated and known a bit about Vietnam. I withstood this, primarily with the assertion that after the politicians and critics had had their say, still an officer had to take care of his men.

Mind you, I am now getting to my first priority in retirement. This La Costa meeting, and you might say, the start of a new life, actually took place some weeks before my San Diego retirement parade and while I was still in uniform. Things really got underway there at La Costa when, not having a coat and tie that were called for in the dining room, I borrowed same and thus could escort Else in for dinner. My wife had not come up with me from Coronado.

Else's heritage was Danish, and I quickly received an education in the matter of all things about that stalwart nation. As a matter of fact, I was to take a course for credit at UCLA, for which the most liberal professor required papers on a minority populace or fringe community. That did not seem to literal-minded George that I was necessarily obligated to write on some oppressed, put-upon, out-of-the-main-stream, people or nation. Small Denmark qualified naturally in a mathematical count. It was my minority now, no matter what the prof felt. His attitude was that you must chose and have to write about victims of racial prejudice, the poor, the downtrodden—*his* minorities.

Else's mother Hilda had come from the city of Logstor in northern Jutland, where North Sea winds and weather indeed made life hard but people sturdy. She had followed an older relative to the United States as a nurse in WW I. Originally she might have been involved in nurturing tuberculosis patients into the beneficial climate of Southern California. She was also commissioned as a nurse in the U.S. Army, but scarcely ever seemed to realize what this meant. It seemed that there had been a return-to-Denmark plan in her future, but Else's very imminence caused a permanent postponement of that return. She stayed Old World most of the rest of her life, never wanting to board a ship or an airplane, and Los Angeles came to be her home for her proud career as a nurse and mother.

Else's father Holgar also came from Logstor, actually a spot nearby with the nifty name of Windblaes (Wind Blazes to me). He was selected by the town elders for education as a doctor at Copenhagen University. It was the Danish practice that a young man be sent for his education, as a doctor, teacher, preacher or perhaps even lawyer, from the town in order that he return to serve the community. Unfortunately, Kaiser Wilhelm's Germans interfered in his plans during an August 1914 visit to Heidelberg, another great institute for learning and medical studies. Holgar boarded a ship in Amsterdam, hoping to get home, but instead found himself transported to Canada as war broke out. He joined the Canadian regiment of the Scottish Black Watch Highlanders, the "Ladies From Hell," saw the war and too much of it from the trenches of Flanders: and ended up after a Canadian discharge, in the United States. The horror and dislocation of war had spoiled his plan for a medical career. Instead he found Hilda and gave life to Else in Los Angeles. I never knew him, but I respect his achievements as an educated man, a leader of Danes in California, and editor of the Danish paper, *Bien.* He was a blithe spirit who spoke many languages and took delight in a hobby of collecting Greek and Roman coins.

*   *   *

It was not to be some slinking off to a justice of the peace in Las Vegas, but a celebratory occasion in and of the best that Denmark might offer. Else's cousin had been a golfing partner with the queen and this led to the privilege of marriage in the royal chapel in Fredensborg, the site of the monarchs' summer palace. Else's U.S. and Danish relatives were present, and most importantly, Alex, the son whom I was to adopt. I was able to command appearance out of Paris by Ernie deZaldo, my preppie friend from Cuba; Larry Brody, out of London, my comrade from Yale and the Marine Corps; Lt. Col. Fred Rohde, the pilot for General Taylor, then on NATO assignment in country; and Danish friends of my parents. Best of them all was my first cousin, Graydon Rogers, the best man, a colonel of the British Staffordshire Regiment whose blue uniform was remarkably like mine. The dinner that followed the ceremony was an unforgettable, formal, not black-tie but white-tie, affair. Ernie, the bachelor, was a charmer to the bridesmaids. Larry, one-legged after combat at Tinian, reminded all of what military service sometimes might exact. Cousin Graydon supplied great hilarity.

What do couples do after a wedding? No, I mean, what about the honeymoon? Newlyweds usually go on a trip. Where did we venture? It was spring of the year, and we had to get out of rainy Copenhagen, so we booked a cruise of the Aegean on a small Greek ship. I now mention the first of many trips and cruises we were to make after my time in the Marine Corps. I was surely impelled into these by my passion for geography; I wanted to journey to places I had never been before. When there I had to know in which directions the rivers flowed, where highways led, and where borders lay. On this honeymoon cruise we made Crete, a cradle of civilization, as yet untroubled in a serious way by Greek and Turkish differences. We stopped at the interesting islands of Mykonos, Santorini, and Lesbos. On Good Friday we participated in the spiritual and reverential atmosphere of a small islet close to Athens. Next night was the occasion of a solemn and important midnight procession downhill to the central heart of the Greek Orthodox Church. This was during the era of the hegemony of the Greek colonels, so the spiritual impact of the parade was spoiled by the participation of several, jack-booted police or soldiers, weaving to and fro aboard their motorcycles, with flashing, roaming blue headlights. We departed Athens on a rather last-minute, peculiar flight arrangement—a Bulgarian Airlines plane, with lots of yogurt, via Bengazi, to Tunis. The bonus there was the tourist opportunity to see the Roman ruins of Carthage. And seeking to entertain my bride, we attended a soccer game in a large stadium in Tunis, where Else found herself the only lady present, pretending interest in soccer. Back to California on Air France via Paris.

*　　*　　*

I was now remarried, a responsible groom and become a father—but how about a job, a next career, what to do with our futures? Actually I had found employment as a computer programmer at the telephone company, before the leave had been requested and trip made for our wedding in Denmark. I had shifted my interest from perhaps becoming a history teacher into this

186

world of computers. I wanted to catch up on a younger generation and new mathematics. I added some qualifications learned at the University of California by attendance at night school, computer-programming courses. There was a referral on my behalf from that San Diego school I had attended, and a successful interview by the General Telephone Company of California. I was older than most of my associates and found myself at a disappointingly low level on the scale of responsibility and performance, a comedown after my Marine years.

Yet it gave me dignity and preoccupation over a couple of years, during which I got used to Beverly Hills, supported Else in our new lives, and adopted Alex. I never comprehended what my true duties at the phone company were or could be. I composed some programs on Hollerith punch cards and debugged others in COBOL, the computer language of that day. Oddly I got myself involved in problems over redesign of the automobile parking facilities for the General Telephone Company and what to do about the high degree of heat generated by the machines in the processing room. There was a myriad of reports then required, at wildly different times or intervals, by various company and branch offices or desks. Some were due weekly: some on the 15th day of the month, some only in case of a shortage or mistake, some requiring massive, unnecessary accounting. I had a fling at composing a report on reports. Looking back I think there was too much reporting on everything, so much that the processing rooms ran too long, generating that heat. Others did something about that, by getting printouts of only the exceptions, shortages, mistakes, or faulty billings, rather than the total mass. I confess that I frequently wasted time in reading the newspaper, but deny that I was in sympathy with the startling lengthy coffee breaks my colleagues took every morning and afternoon. I also admit that I worked the company pretty strongly for vacations and even extra time off. I valued the chance for that job. It was a better choice than trying to break into the educational hierarchy. I was probably squeezing into a structure at too low a level. Forgive me for the wisecrack that I make about leaving General Tel, "I was in charge of wrong numbers."

*   *   *

I successfully gravitated into Beverly Hills life, particularly a charming home in the hills. Physically the scene included coyotes, which broke in under our chain-link fence to get a drink out of the swimming pool. Deer would flee out of the road in front of our home on Hidden Valley Road. I loved the coo of doves and hooting of owls. And we even had, though only one of each—an aged turtle, a very large raccoon, and a rattlesnake. That last required young Alex to pin it down and me to decapitate. You should have seen how it writhed in the trash container for hours later. I tried walking through the hills, through wilderness surrounding the reservoir, on my way to a tennis game, and caught an all-time case of poison oak.

I found myself in the center of buoyant, expansive Los Angeles with its wonderful cultural, social, athletic, and educational opportunities. Downtown was an easy jaunt away, although the number of automobiles on freeways and accordant polluted air is distressing and depressing. Over the years we have enjoyed theatre and music, principally in Los Angeles' superb Music Center. We were in the hills, so when I descended south I could be a hotshot in the pleasures of Beverly Hills, the heart of the entertainment industry, meaning movies. I'll entertain now by a name-dropping of some of my neighbors, variously and over time—Charlton Heston, Candace Bergen, Angie Dickinson, Julie Andrews, Rex Harrison, Walter Matthau, and Jack Nicholson—while remarking that I might be called the sheriff of Hidden Valley Road.

Alex came along with Else when he was a ten-year-old so I soon undertook the adoption process. With the boyhood that I had been through, for me his education was an important priority. Private school? Well, OK, and Else agreed. I know my impact and outward appearance must have been overwhelming for Alex, as I entered his life. It's possible, however, that I saved him from certain pitfalls in the excesses of Beverly Hills. And there was still more to come in his educational path. Alex has become a proud, achieving, and responsible police officer in Idaho, making an escape from the "life of captivity" in which he found himself. My road had been the military, but I claim that Alex has meaningfully emulated me in his choice of a career to protect law and order.

Else had nurtured me into acceptance and participation in California. In fact, I trust she will forgive me as I assert that sooner or later in our early conversations a reference to Denmark or Southern California would crop up. Early in our marriage she encountered Charlton Heston, and what do you know?—he was the same good movie star that I had escorted in Danang, where he had been cheering the troops. Later circumstances prompted Chuck to get me up to his home and tennis court on a ridge above Hidden Valley Road. I have been his pal in the weekend games there ever since. The Los Angeles Tennis Club, historic home for the southwest's biggest yearly tournament, has also been a most pleasant discovery.

I like to say that athletics kept me out of the bars, so there was also golf to keep me on a straight course. I was not very proficient at the game, but I got my son Alex off onto a great start. I could not find reliable partners. So for a few years, pretty much alone, I would try Los Angeles' many public courses. Then, when you might say I had earned it and could afford it. I joined Bel Air Country Club, a true treasure for me and not far from home. This is the heart of moviedom, and I see the great and near great about me. The theatre and music are available more importantly for me than cinema, so I follow Else's lead in the matter of movies. And she is properly critical here, having grown up in this city. This has been a reporting of mere trivial pursuits, but soon to come was a geographical turn of events in an historical setting that represented another big change in my life.

*   *   *

In the summer of 1972 we signed up for a summer school opportunity sponsored by the University of California, Berkeley, conducted at Worcester College, Oxford, and it turned out to be sort of a reconnaissance, a testing of the waters, to what I might want to pursue later. I had built up a pretty good head of steam on the history of foreigners who went to Formosa in the 19th century, but I could not plan a dissertation subject for the Ph.D. degree in my home in Beverly Hills. Neither did the courses offered that summer at Worcester College relate to my field of interest, but we flourished in the atmosphere and blandishments of life in Oxford and the Costwolds. I recall one little discussion with a very able, competent, lady professor of English history. She asserted that, of course, the class system had vanished in England. Well, maybe, but one might better say that it had been reformed. And I, seeing other aspects of British social life, practices, and the culture, was bound to argue—no, there were many remnants still of the class system about us. Pay attention, Lords and Ladies.

We enjoyed nearby Stratford and Shakespeare, London and lucky times for a day at Wimbledon, and Folkestone, Kent, with that Brit cousin, colonel, who had so recently played the part of best man, in Fredensborg, Denmark. I wandered about among Oxford faculty members, seeking one who might sponsor me for a China dissertation. First was a scholar in the poetry of ancient Chinese dynasties. He and I lived in different worlds. However, he introduced me to two outstanding, amiable professors who advised me to go ahead and apply for admission to St. Antony's College. Geoffrey Hudson and Richard Storry were to become my friends and mentors in time to come. Yet, they were both accomplished in the history of Japan, not China. Well, that was close, but did not exactly meet my target.

In addition I encountered two Yank pals, both former Marines, both finished and proven scholars, and both ready to tell a lot of stories and to join a party. Bob Asprey had been a WW II vet, recalled to active duty in Korea time to my very office in G-2, HQMC. His field was Germany and France. In years to come he achieved prominence as a historian with acclaimed biographies on Frederick the Great and Napoleon. The other was none other than Gen. Sam Griffith, living in the walls of Blenheim Palace, and at this time working on the American Revolution, as seen in the eyes and records of the British. More importantly in my measure, he had been a Chinese language student in Peking, had translated and written on Sun Tze, the Chinese god of war, and on Mao Tse-tung. He had commanded a battalion of USMC raiders on Guadalcanal and had been helpful to me back in 1945, when I struggled to stay in Tsingtao, China, vice being shipped to Guam.

Else and I returned to Beverly Hills after this initial summer course full of enthusiasm for England and Oxford, so we made plans for a big return and formal admission to the University. Oxford had a system, difficult for Yanks to understand, that one gained admission to a subordinate college before acceptance by the University itself. The lady admissions officer of St. Antony's showed little interest in me, with the declaration that I did not have much of a chance, that only about one in 35 applicants would get in. I sensed that this was a bit of an exaggeration, and it came to pass that Professors Hudson and Storry ensured my admission.

In passing let me add this. An American arriving at one of our graduate schools generally has questions about courses, teachers, which dormitory, what is your scholarship program, schedules, teams, and extra-curricular interests. At Oxford they simply say, "Get in the library, boy; write a book, and contribute something to man's knowledge. You teach us." Another little detail that cropped up was that a student was supposed to live within ten miles of

Carfax, from the French "carrefour" for crossroads. This was an ancient ruling to inhibit dilettantes from pretending they were serious about Oxford while actually enjoying a playboy's life in distant London. In my case it threatened an idyllic solution to our living arrangements, already made, but the restriction was quickly overlooked when I indignantly protested.

*　　*　　*

I still had a flavor in me of the military, so let me consider the next things to come from the general staff point of view. The personnel were lined up—I myself; Else, who completed some work at the University of Southern California so she could participate academically; Alex, who was admitted to a "public" school, not easily set up but later proven ideal; and Rover, my beloved Lhasa Apso. I could not bear to leave him behind, so I engineered his lonely, forlorn departure on a hot afternoon at L.A. airport, destined for the required six-month incarceration for quarantine in a Gloucestershire kennel.

The intelligence considerations had been met. I knew the challenge ahead of me. I knew more about modern China than did the lineup at St. Antony's, Geoffrey Hudson and Richard Storry both being specialists on Japan. Operational planning was in order, with an ambitious trip from California to Oxford, via Alaska, Siberia, and Moscow all arranged. The logistics presented minor problems. There had been a mail strike in Britain, so I did not definitely know whether or not I had been admitted during the several weeks of planning on leaving Beverly Hills. Leasing our Beverly Hills home and loading seven trunks were not minor problems. Then, help me, there was a shipping strike! We three were to exist out of suitcases in a foreign country, in approaching winter, with housing and locomotion challenges to be dealt with. We all deserved medals.

For the Oxford venture we undertook an unusual direction

192

and itinerary of travel. U.S. airlines had been given little consideration for scheduled flights to the Soviet Union, and the Russians chose first to award a franchise to Alaska Airlines, for the flights from Juneau to, well, whatever. We made Khabarovsk, named for the first Russian seriously to expand the empire to the Siberian Far East. Now we transferred to Aeroflot, the Russian airline. Then Irkutsk, where one could take a swim in the deepest, greatest volume of water, of lakes, in the world.

The flight stewardesses were better educated in art history and Christian history than we passengers were. On one front, however, I was taken up short. After Alma Ata and Samarkand, without a map in front of me and just trying to visualize where we were and were going. I asked where was that railroad route in from Persia. Answer: there is no such thing nor was there ever a railroad in from, well now call it Iran. I protested that indeed there was—you know, the route over which the West sustained Russia during WW II with Lend Lease supplies? You know, the help that enabled the Soviet Union to withstand Hitler? Well, I got back that there was no such thing as Lend Lease. The glorious, heroic, workers, and soldiers of Marx and Lenin had stood alone, without any help whatsoever from the decadent, capitalist Western allies. By this time, having fallen, Joseph Stalin was no longer to be mentioned. He was gone from the history books and conversational exchanges. There was little sense to discuss a mere railroad line.

The tour continued to Sochi on the Black Sea, where there was a touch of feeling of Armenia. Then St. Petersburg, a magnificent destination for tourists. At Moscow we cut loose from our tour group, which continued with a small loop around the North Pole en route back to Alaska. Thus passengers could say they had circled the globe. I could say I'd been there, around the belly of the earth, done that. Next, Prague and East Berlin. It is a silly claim, but hereafter we could say we'd been in East Berlin, but never West.

*   *   *

The Russians had been pleasant to us, but it was with a tremendous feeling of relief that we boarded British Air with our ponderous load of suitcases for England. First objective was to get Alex to his school, near Banbury, and to solve the housing problem. It was initially a grim task but we stumbled into a sweet cottage in the village of Eastleach Turville, enabling easy introduction into Cotswolds life. Our landlady was a descendant of both Charles Darwin and Joseph Wedgwood. Her husband was a veteran of the civil service in India, a past director of the Wedgwood firm, and a true liberal and aristocrat. The only thing I can say is that I would never recommend a similar objective in England, Oxford, to another. He could never come close to matching our good fortune.

*   *   *

It was a bit of a struggle to purchase an automobile, and the very second-hand Ferrari was a disaster. It had 12 cylinders, and a bank of six would frequently all fail at the same time. I eventually peddled it off on a Texan who was engaged in an oil terminal development in Wales. (I doubt that it lasted until he could take it home.) In a final recitation of difficulties, not a real complaint, I daily commuted a triangular course. I would ease Alex's transition by a dawn trek to his new and unfamiliar school; continue to St. Antony's at Oxford for the D.Phil. pursuit; get back to our Cotswolds, where Else waited; and finally make the round-trip journey to Banbury to get Alex home for bed. We could not keep this up for long. Alex boarded. I got going with my research. And I could be most solicitous and caring for Else, sort of marooned but still enjoying our treasured home in the most idyllic of scenes and with greatest of friends.

Academically I steamed along rapidly utilizing the Bodleian and St. Antony's libraries at Oxford and at London's Public Record Office. I knew about the modern history of Taiwan, had lived there, and had studied earlier on the Impact of the West upon China. As a generality it must be conceded that the foreigners intruded into the island to peddle opium, conduct gunboat diplomacy, interfere in sovereignty, and push the missionary drive of Dominican Catholics and English Presbyterians. I spoke passable Mandarin Chinese and was seriously interested in the island. I was pretty much on my own in composing my dissertation, "Foreigners in Formosa, 1842–1874."

At weekly interviews with my tutor, I fear that Geoffrey Hudson often just fell asleep. He voiced one theory, however, that I have not forgotten. He offered that Christianity had quickly vanished in Japan and had made only a small foothold in China. So, he held, do not think that communism, another ideology of the West, would have any more lasting meaning for China. It might be gone, comparably with the missionary movement in China, in a blink of the eye of history.

I volunteered to lead seminar periods on the Far East. The atmosphere at St. Antony's was respectful for this Vietnam veteran, but I had two encounters out of the ordinary with other Americans. A St. Antony's student, younger than I and with no experience in Asia, verbally attacked me, in protest over the war in Vietnam. Perhaps I agreed with him in part, but I knew that my involvement had been to take care of my men.

Another meeting was that of Else and me on a tour of one of England's stately mansions, open one day a week to the admiring public. We observed two American ladies, who showed interest in my studies and service in Vietnam. This time I might have intended to criticize policy, tell of the impossibilities of campaigning there, and maybe even offer a caveat, "Never get into a land war in Asia." However, the two ladies were sisters, one being the wife of Admiral McCain, then the very commander of our forces in the Pacific. And we all know of her son, Comdr. John McCain, then a prisoner of the cruel Viet Cong in solitary confinement near

Hanoi. I, of course, kept my mouth shut about Vietnam policy to her. Today I salute the gallant senator from Arizona. I have no sympathy for that student war protestor, who was then probably in any case evading the draft.

*　　*　　*

In the traditional ceremony I was awarded that degree from Oxford, and we returned home to Beverly Hills. I was glad that we did not keep Alex any longer out of his home grounds. A little more time in England, and would he know whether he was a Yank or Brit? We made the decision to send him off on another new, educational challenge—entry into the Marine Military Academy, a private, boys', military, boarding academy, in Harlingen, Texas, in the delta of the Rio Grande. I intend the MMA story to be a highlight, the climax, to my journey as a Marine. Alex had endured quite a series of jumps—Beverly Hills elementary school, an exposure to private school elsewhere in California, the trans-Atlantic leap to Banbury, and now back in his own country, to this Marine Military Academy in Harlingen, Texas.

I kept busy for a time in California trying to help a friend and neighbor, Alphonzo Bell, a longtime congressman in his campaign for senator from California. He did not make it. But it was a fulfilling and satisfying effort, in a field new to me, to try to put him across. Too, I was concerned with what might come next for me. Could I get somewhere in the field of education with my Oxford degree? Maybe become a public school principal, or headmaster of a private school? I sensed that I was overeducated and anyway no one in those days, in that atmosphere seemed receptive to bring a retired colonel, tainted with Vietnam, to run a school for his children.

*　　*　　*

In turning to my final period of a military career, I have other tales to tell, trips to recall, and interesting geographical places to present. I cannot overlook them, minor and insignificant though they be, so bear with me as I continue to move on. We all know that the future is more important than the past, and I have often declared that I forget what I have done, but I always know what I'm going to do next! However, inconsistently I shall never forget some of the adventures that I enjoyed in retirement. In fact, I'd like to do all of them all over again.

I once had the opportunity to visit Haiti, where U.S. Marines had repeatedly served in attempts to bring order and stability. I had an introduction by a Haitian who asserted that his own profession was that of a private investigator or detective and that he had an important cousin, a peace officer in Port-au-Prince. The cousin readily volunteered to take me on a reconnaissance trip of the countryside outside the city. I was interested in visiting the fabled Mellon Hospital, perhaps the only viable medical institution in that country. It was said that it succeeded in its enterprise by its location outside in the country and most of all, by staying clear of all political and/or governmental affairs. Medicine and religion in Haiti both had a touch of voodoo, maybe good for Haitians but strange to outsiders. Madsden, an import-export firm (a Danish company, what else?) seemed to manage the only economic enterprise in the country. Madsen's head officer told me that his children not only went for their education in Florida, but also that a small pool of children in Haiti was officially, technically, fully, a subordinate part of the Miami school system. We did not get far on our automobile trip.

The purported high peace official had to beg for gas for his empty tank, and as we departed, had to ignore the shrieks of his Brooklyn-born and raised wife, who seemed to fight and ridicule him on all fronts. The roads in Haiti were all-time miserable, despite the fact of U.S. aid appropriations. As dark approached, we had a flat tire, and sure enough, no spare. I was dispatched to beg help from a neighborhood that was enthusiastically entertained by our breakdown. Later, we attempted to ram some rubber bands into the tire hole, but were interrupted by a truckload of scornful, derisive soldiers, who stopped to laugh at us. They peed on me. The Tonton Macoute glowered as we left the island, and that only after a big squabble with the airline, which had canceled, lost, or resold my reservation for home.

Else and I enjoyed several wonderful summer trips to Europe, particularly back to the British Cotswolds and to Denmark's Jutland. We also visited and toured in France, Italy, and Spain. On these jaunts we often capitalized on the opportunity of space-available air travel. Retired personnel could get free flights when the space was available. I recall a lift from Taiwan to Korea, where arriving unexpectedly the only accommodation we could manage was in the spare room of an apparent brothel. We once flew from England over Scotland, watching air refueling of a Strategic Air Command aircraft on which we had bummed a ride, en route to Iceland. We also enjoyed this space-available privilege after a long cruise on a French liner, a visit to enchanting Bali, and a long leg back from Guam to California.

When we resided in the Cotswolds, we were close to Brize Norton, a primary Royal Air Force base, and Fairford. Fairford had been a WW II field, had been enlarged for the development of the Concorde, was actually a USAF facility but under a British flag, and the site of Britain's annual air show. It was an especially handy spot for me to qualify for flights.

We made Panama, from which we traveled by bus to visit friends in Costa Rica. At the military's golf course in Panama I encountered a soldier who had been one of the party at Panmunjom attacked by the North Koreans, killing a U.S. Army major with an axe. An inconsequential meeting, but meaningful for me. From Costa Rica we returned to Van Nuys, California, airfield by the Wyoming Air National Guard. It sounded odd, but air guard units were important for supporting Central American, U.S. embassies those years in those unstable times.

Our retirement adventures also included the Mediterranean, so I tell of an episode on board *Mermoz,* a small French cruise liner. The voyage was billed as a "Jules Verne Round The World" trip, but indeed was only from Marseilles via the Suez and Panama Canals, the Pacific, for repositioning for the Caribbean winter trade. It was a lengthy trip, taking us from Marseilles to Bali. A bonus was that I learned how to play bridge using the French language. To include Cairo on the itinerary required a bus ride to and from Port Said. When we returned to that port, there was an atmosphere of great excitement and turmoil. The port officials carefully interrogated each of us re-boarding passengers, specifically identifying us for *Mermoz.* The captain was insisting on an immediate night departure for the Canal and the Red Sea. It turned out that the other ship in port had been *Achille Lauro,* captured by terrorists who had thrown overboard a helpless wheelchair passenger. Next day for us the air was filled with aircraft, hastening to the scene not only for *Achille Lauro* but also for the escaping terrorists flying via Sicily to Libya or Tunisia.

*   *   *

One day, returned from Oxford and only intermittently busy with helping Al Bell in his campaign for senator from California, I answered a phone call from a certain Col. Bill Card. He was a former running mate, also an artillery officer, an important veteran of combat in North Korea, who was then serving as commandant of cadets at the Marine Military Academy. Alex being a student there, it was not surprising that the school should think of me as a possible replacement as the academic dean. (I preferred to call the position, "headmaster.") I also had another pal in town, Orrin Johnson, who had been a fellow officer on Bougainville, Guam, and Iwo with us, and had returned to Harlingen to be the outstanding lawyer in town. He was one of the founders of the school and later was to be head of the Texas Bar Association.

199

Bill was sounding me out in behalf of the superintendent, Gen. George Bowman. I had last known him in years at HQMC, so the upshot was that Else and I took a trip to have a look around. This was a challenge and opportunity that I could not turn down. After all, the purpose was education; the beneficiaries were very deserving young men, and the atmosphere was reflective of that most important institution in my life, the Marine Corps. I had not found a comparable occupation and solution for my future in Southern California. I know it was sort of a concession on the part of Else, abandoning California for Texas, but it brought us close to Alex again.

The school was located in Harlingen, near Brownsville in the delta of the Rio Grande. It had been founded by the individual effort of an enterprising former Marine. He had a dream, but where was he to locate and organize the academy? The story is that Lyndon Johnson, once campaigning at the airfield in Harlingen, had been greeted by a group that—well, looked at things differently than he. They carried a black coffin on which was emblazoned, "Died in 1946. Voted for Lyndon Johnson in 1948." He was so irate that he had the airfield closed as a federal facility, and it became available as an ideal site for MMA. Notably the old officers' club could become the mess hall for cadets, but there was a formidable amount of cleaning up, new construction, and improvement of facilities, before an actual school could be opened. The "living was easy" for us, finding a rental home next to the Harlingen Country Club. We made friends, explored nearby Matamoros, played bridge and golf, and were not far from the vacation spot of South Padre Island.

General Bowman and Bill Card and I strove mightily in these times to build the school. The faculty was small but competent and dedicated. I am proud that I hired the first female teacher. She was very important, capable in many fields of study, lightening the atmosphere especially for the youngest cadets. Enrollment was below one hundred. We sought to attract more students, but perhaps it might have been easier were we located closer to a major city. Most cadets entered from Texas cities, and we had several boys from Mexico. There were minor problems. Some parents were unable to keep up on the bills, and accordingly we had to squeeze out scholarship funds to help a boy continue. My four primary faculty stalwarts for Math, English, Science and Languages performed magnificently, but there was a turnover in faculty from year to year. Football was big in Texas, so we had to keep up in that field. Some of the Mexican lads were beginners in English, but old enough for the 12th grade. The Drill Instructors, being the pillars of the military side of MMA, were impressive, grandfatherly models for our cadets. Sometimes a student felt he could give more attention to, strive to please his DI, than he could to his teacher. Bill Card and I enjoyed a profitable rivalry—he pushing the military side and I, the academic.

Alex moved on from MMA, Else and I had achieved and successfully met our challenges, so the MMA chapter was closed and we returned to California. Inevitably, this sounds as if it were sort of a sorry ending, a dribbling away, a mournful farewell to a career. The Chinese have an expression, "Head of a Dragon, the Tail of a Snake." For me the dragon is the image of my life, career, achievements, adventures, happiness, and successes. The tail of the snake, vanishing underneath a door, is disappearance, dejection, anticlimax, the end. My Escape from Captivity had been glorious. The Head of the Dragon proclaims his abiding victories. Never was there any tail of a snake for this Marine.

About the Author

George W. Carrington, born in 1921 in New York City, is a colonel, U.S. Marine Corps, (ret.), and a Chinese linguist and historian who attended the Hotchkiss School in the 1930s and went on to earn advanced degrees from Yale, American, and Oxford Universities. The author participated in the campaigns of World War II, Korea, and Vietnam; saw duty in Tientsin, Peking, and Tsingtao; trained Chinese marines and served as assistant naval attaché in Taiwan. Colonel Carrington also filled peacetime assignments in Headquarters Marine Corps, Washington, D.C., and in Camp Lejeune, North Carolina. He served as aide to General Maxwell D. Taylor, chairman of the Joint Chiefs of Staff during the Kennedy and Johnson administrations. His academic career has included graduate teaching at San Diego State University; filling the post of dean at the Marine Military Academy, in Harlingen, Texas; authoring *Foreigners in Formosa, 1841–1874*; and serving as editor and author of the Introduction to *Through Peking's Sewer Gate: Relief of the Boxer Siege, 1900–1901*. Married with a grown son, the author's hobbies include athletics, the study of history, and enjoying geography through maps, stories of exploration, and actual travel. He and his wife reside in California.